*PrincetonReview.com*

# COMPLETE GUIDE TO COLLEGE APPLICATION ESSAYS

### By the Staff of The Princeton Review

Penguin
Random
House

The Princeton Review
110 East 42nd Street, 7th Floor
New York, NY 10017
E-mail: editorialsupport@review.com

Published in the United States by Penguin Random
House LLC, New York, and in Canada by Random House
of Canada, a division of Penguin Random House Ltd.,
Toronto.

Some of the content in *Complete Guide to College
Essays* has previously appeared in *College Essays That
Made a Difference,* published as a trade paperback
by Random House, an imprint and division of Penguin
Random House LLC, in 2014.

ISBN: 978-0-525-57017-2
ISSN: 2692-2606
eBook ISBN: 978-0-525-57027-1

The Princeton Review is not affiliated with Princeton
University.

Editors: Aaron Riccio and Anna Goodlett
Production Editors: Liz Dacey and Emma Parker
Production Artist: Deborah Weber
Content Contributors: Corinne Dolci, Devery Rae Doran,
Brad Kelly, Julia Moody, Jason Morgan, Rita Williams

Printed in the United States of America.

10   9   8   7   6   5   4   3   2   1

First Edition

## Editorial

Rob Franek, Editor-in-Chief
David Soto, Director of Content Development
Stephen Koch, Survey Manager
Deborah Weber, Director of Production
Gabriel Berlin, Production Design Manager
Selena Coppock, Managing Editor
Aaron Riccio, Senior Editor
Meave Shelton, Senior Editor
Christopher Chimera, Editor
Anna Goodlett, Editor
Eleanor Green, Editor
Orion McBean, Editor
Patricia Murphy, Editorial Assistant

## Penguin Random House Publishing Team

Tom Russell, VP, Publisher
Alison Stoltzfus, Publishing Director
Amanda Yee, Associate Managing Editor
Ellen Reed, Production Manager
Suzanne Lee, Designer

# Acknowledgments

This book would not have been possible without the aid of the many individuals who helped to assemble and streamline the wealth of information within. We want to thank William Floyd for his early contributions to our outlines and research, and Corinne Dolci, Devery Rae Doran, Brad Kelly, Jason Morgan, and Rita Williams for their ability not only to deliver top-notch strategies and content but to do so under the added pressure of the changes to the work environment in the midst of COVID-19. We'd also like to recognize the contributions of the students and admissions officers who were willing to give us a peek behind the curtains of their work. And of course, an extra special thank you to Julia Moody, who graciously contributed the expertise that she daily brings to our College Admissions Counseling division to this print title, working above and beyond not only to develop chapters for us, but to fact-check and revise other sections as necessary.

Of course, the development of a book is only half the story—when it comes to filling the blank pages, this book would not have been possible without the tireless dedication of our Director of Production, Deborah Weber, and her team of production editors, Liz Dacey and Emma Parker, who double- and triple-checked to make sure we hadn't missed anything. Finally, we'd also like to thank our editors Anna Goodlett, for jumping feet first into this project with eyes wide open for consistency, and Aaron Riccio, for taking the lead on this brand-new title.

# Contents

Get More Free (Content) ............................................................... vi

Introduction .............................................................................. 1

**Chapter 1:** Identifying Your Audience.................................. 5

**Chapter 2:** Finding Your Perfect Topic ............................... 35

**Chapter 3:** Developing Your Essay..................................... 65

**Chapter 4:** Choosing Your Tone......................................... 89

**Chapter 5:** Knowing Your Drafts.........................................115

**Chapter 6:** Finishing Your Application ...............................151

**Chapter 7:** Going the Extra Mile........................................177

**Appendix 1:** Grammar and Writing Tips .............................207

**Appendix 2:** Sample of Successful Student Essays ............231

# Get More **(Free)** Content

## at **PrincetonReview.com/guidebooks**

## As easy as **1·2·3**

**1** Go to PrincetonReview.com/guidebooks and enter the following ISBN for your book:
**9780525570172**

**2** Answer a few simple questions to set up an exclusive Princeton Review account.
*(If you already have one, you can just log in.)*

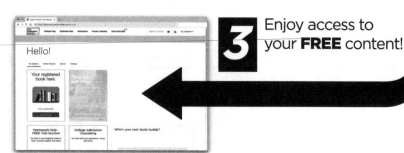

**3** Enjoy access to your **FREE** content!

# Once you've registered, you can...

- Get valuable advice about the college application process, including tips for applying for financial aid

- Use our searchable rankings of *The Best 386 Colleges* to find out more information about your dream school

- Read through a selection of successful sample student essays

- Check to see if there have been any corrections or updates to this edition

## Need to report a potential **content** issue?

Contact **EditorialSupport@review.com** and include:

- full title of the book
- ISBN
- page number

## Need to report a **technical** issue?

Contact **TPRStudentTech@review.com** and provide:

- your full name
- email address used to register the book
- full book title and ISBN
- Operating system (Mac/PC) and browser (Firefox, Safari, etc.)

## Look For These Icons Throughout The Book

 INSIDER TIP

 QUOTE

 CHAPTER REVIEW

 ACTIVITY

 DOs

 DON'Ts

 SUPPLEMENTAL

# Introduction

Welcome to the *Complete Guide to College Application Essays!* Over the many years of our College Hopes and Worries Survey, students just like you have emphasized time and again that completing applications is one of the toughest parts of the college admissions process. But we know that it doesn't have to be! We've spoken with essay readers and application reviewers and we've talked to the experts in our College Admissions Counseling department (https://www.princetonreview.com/college-admissions/college-counseling). We know that there are certain do's and don'ts to this whole process, and we've taken the best advice and strategies surrounding them and distilled it into this book.

In the following chapters, you will find all of the skills you need to get started on your journey from the blank page to the finished essay and application, as well as practical exercises that are designed to get you writing and both actively working and proactively thinking about the road ahead. We use annotated samples to model specifically what works and what should be avoided in essays, and have even included some successful student essays. You'll also find quotes from actual admissions departments that give you some insight into what your eventual readers may be looking for, as well as insider tips from our own experts about what's served applicants in the past. And while there's no substitute for one-on-one mentoring, we'll give you all the tools you need to learn both how to edit your own work and to get the most out of friends and family who might volunteer to help you.

We also strongly encourage you to think of this book as a vital companion to our other admissions guides: *The Best Colleges, Best Value Colleges,* and our online listings if you're still trying to narrow down your list of schools to apply to, *Paying for College* if you're still sorting out what sorts of scholarships or loans might be available for you, and our *Complete College Planner* if you need help organizing the many deadlines on the road ahead. That said, if you're already set on everything but your application—and that's a good position to be in!—let's move right along.

## HOW TO USE THIS BOOK

Just as every writer is different, so too is every reader. While we designed this book to be worked through from beginning to end, we were also faced with the difficult task of designing an essay-writing book that could apply to any student, regardless of whether they were in the home stretch of finalizing their application with one more readthrough or if they hadn't yet written a single word. In short: feel free to skip ahead to whatever section you're currently focusing your work on.

This advice also applies to those of you working through every page. If you run across a brainstorming exercise meant to generate topics or to help select prompts, and you've already done that, don't feel obligated to complete them. That said, it can sometimes help to revisit your ideas with fresh eyes. If you've been stuck for a while, that may be a sign that you need to re-evaluate the choices you've made thus far in your essay. Remember, you're not obligated to use any of the draft work that you complete in this book. You won't be submitting this book along with your application. Just use what you need and leave yourself open to inspiration.

Each chapter begins with an introduction and is then broken into a series of lessons that are supported by engaging, interactive activities designed to do away with writer's block and get you working on your application. We've also provided plenty of annotated examples that serve to model the sort of critical analysis you should be giving your own work, and quotes and tips that emphasize the often-overlooked and neglected essay-writing steps to remain aware of. At the end of each chapter, there's a review activity that aims to allow you to assess your progress so that you can set your own pace. If you're already mid-essay, you might begin using this book by glancing through these reviews to see where you might want to spend more time.

More specifically, here's what you'll find in each chapter:

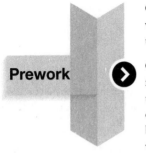

**Chapter 1: Identifying Your Audience** focuses on the ways in which writing a college essay differs from the standard essays you may be used to writing.

**Chapter 2: Finding Your Perfect Topic** begins by looking at the most frequently used prompts—those found on the Common Application—and emphasizes the best practices for breaking down the various questions that will need to be answered. It then provides a series of brainstorming activities and tips for choosing appropriate topics with which to answer those questions.

**Chapter 3: Developing Your Essay** aims to get you producing the initial outline and thesis that will help to ensure that your essay stays on topic as you work on fleshing out each section and fully answering every question. It also walks through the purpose of each part of the college application essay, from introduction to conclusion and, in particular, the need for a captivating opening.

**Chapter 4: Choosing Your Tone** works on refining the core ideas of your essay to help your story stand out, with an emphasis on highlighting formal and informal writing, the importance of sensory details, and the potentially risky use of humor.

**Chapter 5: Knowing Your Drafts** gets deep into the editing process, focusing not only on the work you can do to improve your work and avoid common errors, but on how you can best utilize outside readers and make the most of external feedback.

**Chapter 6: Finishing Your Application** deals with what happens once you've finished the essay—namely, the process for submitting it, and how to potentially minimize the number of applications you'll have to submit for your chosen schools. It also focuses on how to make sure that your essay isn't the only thing that stands out in your application.

**Chapter 7: Going the Extra Mile** highlights some of the additional writing that you may be able to do for your application, whether it's a short-response question, an optional resume, or a letter of recommendation.

At the end of the book, we've provided an appendix of additional good-sense grammar tips to keep in mind, as well as some successful student essays that you can use as motivation.

# GOOD LUCK!

Speaking of tone, although we're very serious about the time-tested strategies that you should be using as you work through the drafts of your essay, we've tried to keep things a little on the light side. The college application process is stressful enough already!

Now, only you know how much time you have before your submission due dates—and if you haven't already written those down somewhere, you probably should. But please be considerate of yourself as you work toward those dates and through this book. Take breaks as needed, and don't be hard on yourself outside of the constructive criticism you give your essay as you edit it. This is hard work, but line by line you're going to get it done, and we'll be here in your corner, cheering you on every word of the way.

# Chapter 1: Identifying Your Audience

## How to Write for a College Admissions Officer

Your college essay isn't like the types of essays you may have written before. It's not meant to demonstrate knowledge of a particular subject, and it's not trying to deep-dive into a research topic. Instead, it's meant to appeal to a specific type of reader—those on the college admissions team!

If you want to get accepted to the college of your dreams, you need to write a successful college essay. The first step is to make sure you're satisfying that target audience.

Okay, you may be thinking, but *how* do I do that? In this chapter, we'll focus on just that—ways to focus your essay so that it appeals not to your teachers, your parents, or your friends, but to your actual audience.

# WHAT YOUR COLLEGE ESSAY ISN'T

Since you've likely written a bunch of essays by this point in your academic career, the easiest starting point is to describe what your college essay should *not* be. Your college essay isn't . . .

- **Written by anyone, for any college**. A college officer wants to get to know *you* and have a sense of how you'd fit into their specific college. Don't submit something generic that could describe any student or any school. Know enough about institution's likely readers so as to write an essay that appeals to them.

- **Written for your friends or family**. The people reading this essay don't know you. So never assume that the reader already knows you or how an event affected you. Plus, remember that the way you tell your story in a college essay is likely very different from how you'd convey it to friends or family.

- **Written for your teachers**. Essays written for a class respond to very specific criteria, for a very specific audience: your teacher. Teachers want you to demonstrate a specific skill you learned in their class and the topics you would use to do so are likely going to be *too* specific for your new target readers in a college admissions office. (Also, remember that admissions officers will also have access to your transcript, GPA, and test scores; you don't need to show off that aspect of your education in your essay.)

## Repurposing the Purpose (of an Earlier Essay)

You don't have to start from scratch when writing your essay. If you've got previously written material that tells a life-changing story or describes something you learned in a class that you're now looking to pursue as a major, you can use such things as starting points. Just because you've written about a topic before does not mean that you cannot use it as a subject for your college essay. You just need to refocus it so that it speaks to your new audience: college admissions readers.

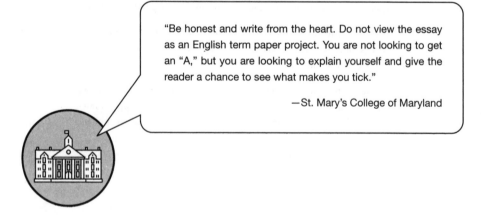

"Be honest and write from the heart. Do not view the essay as an English term paper project. You are not looking to get an "A," but you are looking to explain yourself and give the reader a chance to see what makes you tick."

—St. Mary's College of Maryland

# HOW TO MAKE A REWORK WORK

If you're going to work from pre-existing material, you need to *adapt* it so that it fits your new audience and purpose. (And, though we'll get into that in a later chapter, it of course still needs to answer the essay prompt.) Be critical with your previous content. Ask yourself what it contributes to answering the essay question.

It should convey at least one of the following, depending on the prompt:

- How an experience affected you

- How your outlook was changed

- What caused your plans to shift

- Why your goals are relevant to *their* school

Even if an essay prompt is completely open-ended—and some of them boil down to "write an essay on the topic of your choice"—don't just turn in an essay you completed for a course. It needs to fit the new audience (the admissions team) and a new purpose (getting you admitted!).

That's not to say you write just to tell the admissions folks what they want to hear—not by any means. You can't develop a strong essay if you're just trying to figure out how to get the ball straight into the admissions office's catcher's mitt. Your essay needs to convey your unique story. It just needs to do that by conveying the story to *them*, clearly and memorably.

"Students should express their true voice. There is no right way per se. It may be about a passion or a special interest or a life-changing moment. The challenge is to address the chosen subject with style and substance so that the reader develops a greater appreciation for the writer."

—Earlham College

# A Tale "As Old As Time"

If you're concerned about retelling an existing story to a new audience, take a moment to consider that you've probably already done exactly this, and that you just may not have realized it. Have you ever told a story to one group of friends and then relayed a different version to your parents or to a teacher? Or have you ever texted a shorthand version of something that you then more elaborately described in person?

In March 2020, Grace sent the email below to her best friend Emma. When it comes time to think about her college essay, Grace recalls the image of anxious New Yorkers waiting day after day for COVID-19 testing—and how relieved she was when her grandmother finally got tested after weeks of being afraid to go to the hospital. It was probably one of the most important incidents in life.

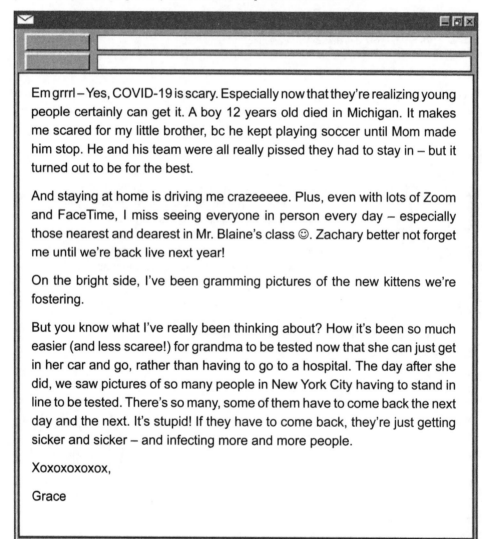

Em grrrl – Yes, COVID-19 is scary. Especially now that they're realizing young people certainly can get it. A boy 12 years old died in Michigan. It makes me scared for my little brother, bc he kept playing soccer until Mom made him stop. He and his team were all really pissed they had to stay in – but it turned out to be for the best.

And staying at home is driving me crazeeeee. Plus, even with lots of Zoom and FaceTime, I miss seeing everyone in person every day – especially those nearest and dearest in Mr. Blaine's class ☺. Zachary better not forget me until we're back live next year!

On the bright side, I've been gramming pictures of the new kittens we're fostering.

But you know what I've really been thinking about? How it's been so much easier (and less scaree!) for grandma to be tested now that she can just get in her car and go, rather than having to go to a hospital. The day after she did, we saw pictures of so many people in New York City having to stand in line to be tested. There's so many, some of them have to come back the next day and the next. It's stupid! If they have to come back, they're just getting sicker and sicker – and infecting more and more people.

Xoxoxoxoxox,

Grace

## ACTIVITY

Now it's your turn. Find a story that you've already told, whether it's an essay you wrote for class, a series of messages you sent to a friend, or even something that you remember telling an acquaintance in person. Provide a version of that in the following space.

_____

_____

_____

_____

_____

_____

_____

_____

_____

_____

_____

## Adapting for a New Audience

Now that you've shared your own version of a story, let's consider how Grace's email to Emma can be translated into an admissions essay for a premed program. Her goal is to explain her passion for biology and medicine.

After brainstorming, she decides that the most relevant part of her story is how to make medical treatment available locally, in order to minimize patient travel. After all, she reasons, if you're sick, you're the one who should be resting comfortably and put at ease, not waiting in line and feeling scared.

Here is the essay she wrote from that experience—using the bare bones sketched in the email as the nucleus of the essay. Please bear in mind that this is not an actual student essay (you can see some of those in the appendix of this book), but rather a sample that shows off the techniques that we're discussing.

Ever since I was little, I've wanted to be a doctor. I used a play stethoscope to hear my dolls' heartbeats and doled out "pills"—baby aspirin—to my teddy bear. I want to be a healer.

But last spring, I realized that, as important as a stethoscope and medication are, there's more to being a healer. I can still remember the intense relief on my grandmother's face when her COVID-19 test results came back negative. She worried for two weeks that her cold and cough meant she was a victim of the coronavirus pandemic, but she was afraid to go to the hospital. She's 82 and it's hard for her to walk. My grandfather was even more scared to accompany her to a big impersonal place they associated with sickness and death.

When drive-through testing started in Washington State, my dad drove both of them. My whole family was happy to have a relatively safe and comfortable way to find out if they were infected—in a familiar car, not in a strange and frightening hospital.

Yet a few weeks later, I saw news that people in New York City were waiting hours in line at a hospital to be tested. Some people had to come back three days in a row. The fear they must have been feeling really hit me. Wasn't drive-through testing available? Or—worse— maybe cars were unaffordable for these potential patients, whose only option then became waiting in line.

COVID-19 made me very aware of how much the way doctors *deliver* medicine matters. After all, I went to my dolls' house and my teddy bear's bed (which was my bed!). What if people develop fatal illnesses just because medical treatment is physically unavailable?

I've long wanted to go to your school because of the excellent premed program. I still do! But now, I also want to go because you offer courses in contemporary challenges in medicine, looking at the sociology and culture of delivery. The conditions we practice in are just as important as medicine itself.

I want to study how we might better serve communities by being in them and thinking creatively about how patients can be served.

Last summer, I worked scooping ice cream in a nearby town. We're by the lake, and everyone wants ice cream after they've been swimming. We get very busy and crowded. But when it got that way, one of my jobs was to pass out a number so it would be first-come, first-serve. So it made me think: could the New York hospital have done that? Passed out numbers every morning, so at least people knew if they had to come back the next day, rather than waiting in line all day?

Or, how about utilizing medical students? Student volunteers can do so much to ease patients' minds. What if medical students had rented a van to take those waiting people to a nearby drive-through for testing, rather than making them wait? Not only would it have helped those patients, it would have eased the burden on the hospital. All the doctors and nurses performing the tests could have been helping patients in the hospital instead.

As I think about wanting to realize my lifelong dream of becoming a doctor, I realize how important it is for me to combine that dream with thinking of new ways to deliver medicine and to help sick and frightened people. The doctors of the future will have to be nimble and mobile to fight epidemics and novel illnesses. I want to be one of them, studying at your school.

Remember, admissions officials want to know how a student will contribute. This indicates how.

It never hurts to be grounded and down-to-earth, and a summer job demonstrates those things!

Here, Grace seals the deal on why she wants to go to this college. She's demonstrating a good fit with the school. Note that you would not normally include this information in a personal essay (unless it was specifically requested).

Evidence of strong problem-solving ability and creativity—two ways the essays indicate Grace will contribute.

Strong close, with a clear statement of fit and goals that should stay with the admissions officers.

Remember that each part of your application serves a specific purpose. A line like this may be great, but likely won't fit in a personal statement, and shouldn't just be shoehorned in.

# ACTIVITY

Now it's your turn—go back to your sample story and do some brainstorming. Answer the following questions:

**What in this story would stand out?**

_____

_____

_____

**What kernels do I want to retain? (Rewrite the important information here.)**

_____

_____

_____

Now, don't write a whole essay just yet, but do take a crack at using what you've found so far to write a clear mission statement specifically to the admissions team.

**What do you want the school to know about you?**

_____

_____

_____

Don't overcomplicate things for yourself. When you start writing your actual essay, give yourself clear-cut building blocks like these and you should be good to go!

# THE ADMISSIONS DEPARTMENT

Right now, you may have an idea for what you *want* to write and where you might pull inspiration from, but perhaps you're still a little unclear on who exactly you're writing for. Let's pull back the curtain on that inner sanctum and talk about the people reading your application.

> "Our readers are all faculty, admission staff, or students. They must have a very strong knowledge of the college and the kinds of students who will thrive here."
>
> —College of the Atlantic

## Who Reads Your Application?

Admissions departments are full of people with strong higher education backgrounds. Admissions officers can be former professors (from your intended major or other departments) or college counselors. Some schools use office staff who specialize in admissions. Some use people specifically trained to read admissions essays. Some colleges also use student readers, for peer-based feedback.

As diverse as these readers can be, all of them share several common traits:

- They are sympathetic to students.
- They are respectful of students and the college.
- *They all want the students they admit to succeed.*

## How Many People Read Your Application?

It's also a good idea to understand that the reading of your essay isn't a one-time thing in most instances. The process varies from school to school—some might have individual readers, some might review it by committees working together, especially for students who are wait-listed. Ultimately, *many* folks are likely to read your essay during the admissions process.

Why are there multiple readings? The primary reason is that while the essay readers are dedicated and strive to fairly judge each essay on its own merits, they're also human. If they personally hate the proliferation of true crime stories on streaming services, they may subconsciously assign a lower score to your essay discussing your Netflix internship—and how it made you want to study the cultural impact of soooo many crime documentaries. Making sure that more than one pair of eyes look over your application helps minimize such subjective responses or unconscious biases.

Multiple readings may also be used to move students among accept/waitlist/deny groups as decisions are finalized.

## What Conditions Are Your Essays Read In?

Let's tiptoe a bit further into that inner sanctum. It's important to know the conditions your essay is read under because it clarifies why your essay has to grab an admissions officer's attention to be successful.

The majority of colleges receive more applications than they can accept. The most selective colleges, like Harvard University, only accept around 5% of their applicants.

Much as they might want to enroll every qualified student, colleges resemble an airplane in one respect. Once all the seats are filled, there's simply no more space. Admissions is the department that decides who fills the seats in the airplane.

To use another metaphor, think of the process as a series of hurdles and your essay as a runner. You might not have to leap over *every* obstacle, but your essay needs to clear more hurdles than those of other students. The colleges you're applying to may have better odds than a 5% admission rate, but it's good to think that critically about your work. If it needed to, would your essay be the one that stood out in a group of twenty?

As you might imagine, admissions officers take their responsibility very seriously. Schools get thousands—sometimes tens of thousands—of essays to read over the course of the season (November to March). They read in a very concentrated way, laser-focused on your essay for up to 30 minutes. Then it's on to the next one—if you don't make an impression, you're going to be forgotten.

# What Are Your Essays Being Read For?

The reason your essay can be handled in such a compressed amount of time is that admissions staff are reading it for certain things. Let's take a deeper look at the elements they look for.

Admissions officers read your essay to find the answers to these three questions:

- Can you do the level of work their college requires?
- Are you a good fit for the school?
- Are you likely to contribute to the school?

## ❶ Can you do the level of work their college requires?

First and foremost, your essay needs to demonstrate that you can do the level of work their college requires. Frankly, it doesn't benefit the college to enroll a student who will be struggling from the start. After all, no one expects the swim coach to put someone on the team who can't already do a decent freestyle, right?

To that end, your essay needs to demonstrate that you are thoughtful, well-organized, and articulate. Your transcript, test scores, and GPA will already be speaking to whether you *can* pass a challenging class; your essay is an opportunity to explain *how* you approach problems or handle work. Remember to use your writing to reveal your process as opposed to describing your results.

## ❷ Are you a good fit for the school?

All schools have a culture. Most have mission (or "value") statements. Admissions officers look to see whether your essay indicates that you'll fit into their culture and mission.

Many people know, for example, that leading science schools like the Massachusetts Institute of Technology (MIT) look for students whose idea of paradise is doing scientific research. Arts-oriented schools like California Institute of the Arts (CalArts), on the other hand, look for creative people whose idea of paradise is cartooning, painting, or playing the marimba.

*Every* school, even those that don't specialize to the extent of the two mentioned above, has a culture and a mission. Research the culture of your chosen schools and use your essay to demonstrate that you are a good fit.

### ❸ Are you likely to contribute to the school?

Admissions officers are thinking about your long-term potential. Not only do they want you to succeed as a student, but they want you to go on to reflect well on them in the future. If they see you now as a smart, motivated applicant, they'll be better able to imagine you as a smart, motivated alumni. Your passion communicates a lot, so try to avoid being lukewarm or tentative in your communications.

It doesn't hurt to talk about contributions you have made and want to continue to make while at college. You can use the mission statement research for this too. A comment like "I know Rice has a great music program, and I want to use my experience as first chair in the all-state orchestra as a starting point for studying violin at your school" powerfully conveys what you can contribute.

## ⟐ SUPPLEMENTAL ⟐

Our attention thus far has been focused on using your personal statement to tell admissions officers what they need to know about you. As a result, we've left out some considerations that are more appropriate for other portions of your application, like supplemental essays. We'll get more into these sorts of submissions in Chapters 6 and 7, but here are some key strategies related to your audience.

## ⟐ Special Circumstances ⟐

At times, the record of student achievement in an application package doesn't tell the whole story. Have you encountered challenges or unusual circumstances? Was your ability to attend school hampered by homelessness, for instance? Or were you not particularly motivated to study, to the degree that your GPA and test scores don't reflect your ability?

A shorter supplemental essay is an ideal space to explain special situations like this, so long as it pertains to the question you're answering. (If given a chance to explain personal challenges, you should write an essay that shares the most about yourself.) In particular, if your motivation or outlook has changed as a result of personal hardship, share the what, why, and how.

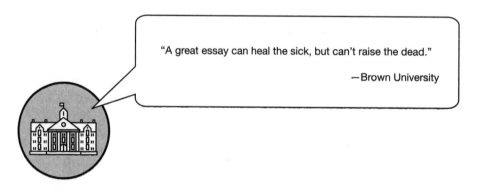

"A great essay can heal the sick, but can't raise the dead."

—Brown University

Admissions officers are fairly understanding, and the more you can demonstrate a shift toward an upward trajectory from here on out, the likelier they are to excuse lackluster grades from an off semester and take a chance on you.

# ✏ School Circumstances ✏

Just as you may want to share special information about yourself, so too do most schools want to share what makes them special. In general, it's a good idea to know what those schools are all about before you get serious with your applications to them, but when it comes to supplemental material, it's specifically a good idea to speak directly to how you'd fit.

The good news is that you don't have to necessarily travel in person to these schools! You can get most of the information you need, especially about a school's mission, from that school's website.

First, analyze the school's website for clues to their culture. Do they show students studying? Partying? Playing sports? Volunteering in the community? Do they emphasize any one of these activities over the other?

Second, look for mission statements. Use a highlighter to focus on keywords. Keywords and other details in the mission statement can tell you a lot about a school, as we show here.

Here's what we found about two very different schools:

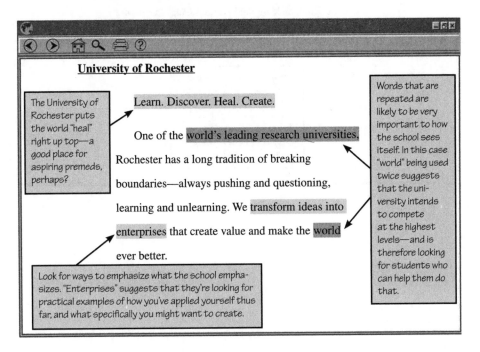

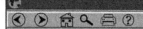

## Oregon State University

That there's an emphasis on Oregon suggests that they value residents and regional applicants. If that describes you, be sure to emphasize your connection to the area in your application.

As a land grant institution committed to teaching, research and outreach and engagement, Oregon State University promotes economic, social, cultural and environmental progress for the people of Oregon, the nation and the world.

This mission is achieved by producing graduates competitive in the global economy, supporting a continuous search for new knowledge and solutions and maintaining a rigorous focus on academic excellence, particularly in the three Signature Areas: Advancing the Science of Sustainable Earth Ecosystems, Improving Human Health and Wellness, and Promoting Economic Growth and Social Progress.

A competitive mission statement implies that the school is looking for competitive students.

Schools will sometimes use complicated course descriptions or program titles. Make sure you fully understand what these are, so that you can speak more directly (and accurately) to them.

This leads us to the next important question you need to ask on this front. Do your current goals fit your school of choice's mission? The more they do, the greater your likelihood of getting in.

While we're at it, be sure to check out the department(s) relevant to your goals. Some schools are strong in geology; others are strong in music. Your fit with a school is helped when you really want to study a topic that the school promotes.

If you visit the school before applying, use your detective skills in a third way. Ask about the culture. Students already at a school are experts on its culture.

Use your detective skills to find out about the school's mission. But never quote the mission statement directly. They know who they are. What they need to learn from your essay is who *you* are.

# ACTIVITY

## Doing Your Detective Work: Getting to Know the Unknowns

The key to any good essay is in giving admissions officers the answers to what they're looking for. But first you need to know the answers yourself, and that means doing a little research.

Pick a school that you're interested in attending. Answer the following three questions:

1. **What level of work does the school expect from students?**
   (You can look at SAT/ACT test-score ranges, average GPAs of admitted students, and samples of work done by first-year students.)

   _____

   _____

2. **What are the school's goals?**
   (Remember to be a culture detective and check their mission statement.)

   _____

   _____

3. **What is the school's culture?**
   (More cultural detective work: contact the admissions office, take a tour, talk to current students.)

   _____

   _____

Now, think about what sort of story your essay could tell that would convey your level of work, your goals, and your cultural fit with the school. How do you relate to each point?

Ultimately, when we ask, "What do admissions officers read for?" the answer is this: a reason to accept you. That's the power of your essay. A great essay can propel the rest of your application forward.

Plus, if your application package places you on the border between admit or don't admit, a well-crafted essay informing admissions officers of your goals, your fit, your potential contribution, your personal circumstances, and why you want to go to their school can make all the difference.

# ACTIVITY

## Grabbing Your Audience

Those reading your personal statement will approach your essay with professionalism and good will, but they need to know, and quickly: Can you do the level of work? Are you a good fit for the school? Will you make a contribution? Have you faced any special situations?

Put yourself in their position. Give yourself five minutes to skim the introductions on the following pages and see what sort of effect those time constraints have on you. Without reading the annotations below each essay, simply rank them from best to worst on the lines below, and write a few words to summarize what jumped out at you, good or bad.

_____

_____

_____

_____

_____

_____

# ESSAY 1

Last year, my great-grandfather died. I loved to hear his stories about World War II. He was one of the soldiers on Omaha Beach during D-Day. One of our favorite things to do together was to watch World War II movies like *Band of Brothers*, *Saving Private Ryan*, and *The Longest Day*.

My favorite scene in the movie is when they are trying to blow up the bridge so the Nazis can't get over it. It shows teamwork and courage. It especially shows Captain Miller's courage but also Private Ryan's courage—Ryan, after all, could have left, but he didn't.

*The Longest Day* is an older movie but it, too, points out the teamwork and courage needed to fight in World War II. It opens on the boats before the soldiers even go over to France. My great-grandfather said that part was realistic; it was aggravating not to know whether they would go or be delayed.

> Which movie of the several mentioned in the paragraph before? Reading further into the paragraph, we can assume that it's *Saving Private Ryan*, but not providing the name makes the essay seem disorganized.

> At this point, the admissions officer might be wondering where the essay is going. It hasn't yet answered a prompt, or indicated much about the student's unique story.

> This essay opens with meaningful events: the death of a loved one and what that loved one and the student liked to do together. But we're now three paragraphs in, and there's no clear indication of what this essay is going to tell the admissions officers about the student.

Essays need organization and pacing. After the opening, the essay shouldn't be a series of smaller moments recounting scenes in movies. It needs to either state what was life-changing or meaningful about the death of the student's great-grandfather, about the joint movie-watching, or about the subject of those movies —and then relate that to the student's desire to attend the college. Is the ultimate point the importance of family ties? History? Teamwork and courage? At this point, it could be any of those, but the student needs to think carefully and decide.

**A Better Idea**: You've got a meaningful life experience here, but think through *how* and *why* it is meaningful to your life trajectory and choice of a college. Then, communicate this to the admissions folks.

# ESSAY 2

The sweet potatoes. The black beans. The tahini sauce. The sage, the parsley, the basil.

Opening with a recital of foods is risky if the essay doesn't reach a point quickly. With this sentence, it does; this is the transformative, unique life story hook.

These are just some of the ingredients that changed my life last year. Before that, I was a typical, hamburger-loving all-American teen. But that was before I realized how much impact our consumption of meat has on climate change. But what do people eat if they can't have hamburgers, steaks, and spare ribs?

Statement of student interest continues to unfold in an engaging way.

My answer is simple: delicious vegan food. The more people eat vegan, the more we save the planet. Working at Sweet Potato Pie, my town's vegan restaurant, was a revelation. The food was not only environmentally healthy, but healthier for people and a wonderful feast to eat.

My goal is to be a vegan cook and restauranteur to educate people about vegan food. You could say I'm pursuing a three-fold path: 1) grab people with great food they'll like; 2) show them how to make it; 3) educate on the importance of the food they like to environmental sustainability.

**A Better Idea**: This is a well-presented introduction to this student's particular passion, but be sure that you commit to a theme for your essay. Splitting between environmental activism, health, and cooking risks presenting a lack of focus.

# ESSAY 3

Epigraphs are risky. You've ceded your first impression to another writer, and you've delayed the action of your essay. Admissions officers tend to see these as filler, so in general, avoid them.

I was a bad kid. I say that without pride.

*Babe Ruth*

This line sounds good—the echo between "sea" and "C's"—and offers a nice contrast with the hard-hitting reality of the next line.

I know the transcript of my sophomore year is a sea of C's and D's. The thing is: I was heavily into drug use that year. I got wasted and didn't study. Once the year was over, my parents sat me down and we had a talk. I wasn't going to get into a good college if my grades didn't improve. My dad said I was ruining my life. I ended up kicking drugs in rehab that summer.

Getting clean was one of the hardest things I've ever done. As you can tell from my much-improved transcript, however, you can see it was totally worth it. If I had been burning bridges before, I hope that now I was rebuilding them stronger than ever. That's why the committee should look at my transcripts from junior high, where the GPA is much higher.

This is a good use of a metaphor to emphasize a shift between two states.

Admissions officers don't like to be told what to do. Give them room to draw their own conclusions: in short, show, don't tell.

**A Better Idea:** Don't write about recreational drug use. And if you do choose to discuss how you turned your life around after some other obstacle, be sure to emphasize the initiative that you took, as opposed to external actions carried out by people like your parents or teachers.

# ESSAY 4

I love movies based on Jane Austen's books. Why? Because they really made me see how my circumstances have been shared by other people—and they chart a way forward. I want to study English and Media Studies to find myself in other books and movies.

What do I mean? Well, from eighth grade until this year, my family was homeless. We moved roughly every three months, often staying in motel rooms. Does motel-hopping in Trenton seem like one of the furthest things in the world from eighteenth-century England? Think again.

In *Sense and Sensibility*, the two sisters and their mother have to move to a much smaller house after a death in the family. They were suddenly much poorer—and it mattered materially. It was the same with my family. My father was in a construction accident and died. My mother's salary couldn't cover the rent. But just as Austen's fictional family pulled through by sticking together and reading together—so too did my family.

> **Immediate statement of goal is great. No admissions officer is going to be at a loss about what the student wants to do!**

> **Straightforward statement of a special circumstance that the admissions officers will find helpful in evaluating the student.**

> **This paragraph gives contextualizing detail about the student's life while also showing an ability to derive meaning and analogies about life from movies and books.**

> **A Better Idea:** The reader might get a better sense of the writer's circumstances if the essay focused more on the financial aspect of having to live on the mother's salary alone, outside of just discussing housing. Likewise, be careful not to use a structure like this—a comparison to eighteenth-century literature—to distance yourself and your readers from the emotional stakes of your journey.

So, now that you've written down which intros grabbed your attention, go back and read the annotations and then see if your list matches up against ours. We ordered these as #2, #4, #1, and #3. Note that our top two work to help the student's chances of being admitted, whereas our bottom two are actually likely to work *against* the student if submitted in this form. Your instincts were likely similar here, so remember to trust your gut. If something doesn't pass muster for *you*, it's almost certainly not going to work for the more critical admissions officers, especially since they'll be unconsciously comparing your work not just to three other essays, but to hundreds.

For the next two intros, try giving some constructive feedback to the authors. On the lines after each, identify whether it's good or bad and, more importantly, explain *why*. For the one that you didn't prefer, see if you can offer a better revision.

# ESSAY 5

I've been fascinated by geology ever since, in the same year, my Mom and I saw lava flowing down the Kilauea volcano in Hawaii and I saw a documentary on Pompeii. The power of nature is awesome—but we need to protect humans from the destructive effects. In Kilauea, they let the lava flow to let the mountain let off steam, in effect. In Pompeii, the volcano blew up and killed hundreds of people before they had a chance to react.

I'd like to learn how to prevent future Pompeiis. The descriptions of people being caught in the middle of eating, or playing with their dogs, are haunting to me. The fact is, towns in Hawaii probably won't be Pompeiis in the future, because of geologists and earth scientists. We have the power to study data on volcanos and make predictions about their danger to human populations. We can move people away from imminent eruptions.

Your college's Geology Department is in the forefront of this study, working with the Decade Volcanoes Project. Last year, I took a course in Earth Sciences where we studied the Hawaiian volcanoes intensively. I would like to continue that study at Your College.

**Did this intro work for you?** _____

# ESSAY 6

If I were to write an essay about the person I most admire in history (and I guess I am!), it's Steve Jobs, because he made a lot of money. (Also, he didn't have to graduate from college to do it!)

Like Steve Jobs, I want to go to college enough to start higher education, but if I see a way to make a fortune before I'm through, I'll be quick to jump into the business world.

I also admire people like Elon Musk. In the future, I'd like to work for his company. He understands that we won't always have drivers in cars and trucks. But I'd like to work on video games that use artificial intelligence too. It's simple: people who are the brains behind AI will eventually run the world. Everyone else will be out of a job.

**Did this intro work for you?** _____

**Take the intro that didn't work for you and try to revise it.** _____

_____

_____

_____

_____

_____

_____

_____

_____

_____

_____

_____

# WHAT EVALUATION SYSTEM DO THE ADMISSIONS OFFICERS USE?

Just as it can help you to visualize who the admissions officers are, the conditions they work in, and what they read for, it can also benefit you to know what system they use when reviewing applications.

Admissions officers have pulled their curtain aside enough to tell us that there are three basic methods:

- Categorization
- Academic Index
- Holistic Method

Let's break that down a bit more.

## Categorization

This method essentially has readers dividing applications into smaller subsets such as definite admits, maybe admits, and rejections. Secondary readers may further shift applications between these piles or serve to narrow down a larger group.

An essay can be one of the factors that moves you between categories. An excellent one demonstrating how much your goals fit with the school might send you from "maybe admit" to the coveted "admit." An essay that shows lack of focus or carelessness, on the other hand, can move you from "maybe admit" to "rejection." All the more reason to put in as much effort as possible in writing the essay.

## Academic Index

Schools that use an Academic Index derive a score from a variety of factors that include things like your GPA and/or class rank, your test scores, and maybe even your SAT subject test scores, although this metric has become less important in recent years. (This index was originally designed to ensure that recruited athletes would be able to perform well academically at the school.) For example, if you had a perfect ACT or SAT score and a perfect GPA, you'd be at the top of the index.

The type of school most likely to use this method is one that's highly selective, wherein they can narrow down the first wave of applications to a subset of only top-scoring students. Only then will they actually read the essays. Keep this in mind before applying; the best essay in the world will do you no good if the school is unlikely to ever read it.

# Holistic Method

Schools using a holistic method look at students, well, holistically. But what does that mean?

High grades are always beneficial. However, schools using a holistic method know that a student is more than just a series of numbers, so you can really make a case for yourself with your essay if your grades aren't as strong as you'd like.

It means those admissions processes focus on you as a whole, 360° person, rather than just as an accumulation of transcripts and test scores. In some ways, the holistic method is the opposite of the index method, which hones in on numerically driven categories. Holistic methods can be highly individual.

Again, it's very important to know what a school values. If it's evaluating applicants in a holistic fashion, it may weigh extracurricular activities above classes, and any special talents you've demonstrated can shine. Schools that require (or highly recommend) an interview and visit are likelier to evaluate students in this way.

To figure out the method that your school of choice uses, you'll have to do some research. Your school counselor may be able to help, and the school itself may give you some hints if you contact their admissions office.

You will likely be at the school you choose for several years. If a school is not forthcoming or transparent about how it operates now, weigh how comfortable you'll be if that continues once you're enrolled there.

There's one thing these methods have in common. All schools will use the essay to help narrow the applicant pool, regardless of how they initially evaluate students. Always put your best foot forward; the story you share may be the deciding factor in your acceptance.

# HOW MUCH WEIGHT DOES THE ESSAY HAVE IN ADMISSIONS DECISIONS?

Your essay will, of course, be part of an application package that includes your transcript, GPA, test scores, and other required material. It's only natural to wonder how important the essay is compared to the other stuff.

Essays are always important, but *how* important depends on what system the school uses and your record. In colleges using a holistic system, your essay can count for a great deal in the admissions decision. In colleges with a categorization system, an essay can move you from category to category.

The admissions staff can use the essay to help determine fit and potential contribution to the school. If the school has a top-rated art program, and you want to be a professional photographer someday, for example, the essay is the place to tell them and make it clear how you fit in.

Colleges that use the Academic Index may weigh numerical and quantifiable measures such as GPA and test scores more highly, but that's not to say that the essay isn't important here. It is. These schools are also looking to determine your fit and contribution, and your essay is a vital component in that decision.

In every school and every system, a lackluster essay can hurt you. Blowing off an essay or skimping on the effort can sink your application. Admissions officers can tell if you've "phoned-in" the essay. It can make them wonder whether you're up to the difficulty level of the school and even make the difference between acceptance and denial.

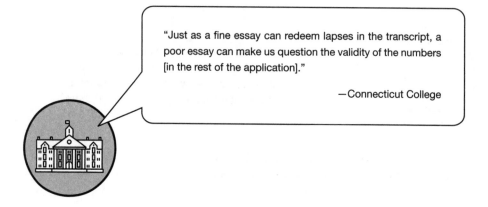

"Just as a fine essay can redeem lapses in the transcript, a poor essay can make us question the validity of the numbers [in the rest of the application]."

—Connecticut College

# AVOIDING POTENTIAL TORPEDOES

Many colleges will give you specific prompts to help guide and focus your essay, or to give you an opportunity to work in details that you want the college to know about you. Some prompts, on the other hand, give you very wide latitude in what to include and how to approach it.

But just because admissions officers give you that leeway, it *doesn't* mean that any topic or approach related to their prompt will satisfy them. In fact, some topics and revelations might actually hurt your chances! You want to avoid sharing anything that could torpedo your chances.

In general, follow the guidance below when choosing what to include in your essay—and what to exclude.

**❶ If you wouldn't discuss it during a job interview or reveal it to your college counselor, it doesn't belong in a college essay.**

Though most admissions officers work hard to remain unbiased and objective when reading an essay, it's a safe bet to assume that some people, even if it's unintentional, [let] their preconceived notions about a topic affect their evaluation of the student writing.

—Cooper Union

**EXAMPLE:** You wouldn't go to a job interview and tell the interviewer that you can't keep off TikTok whenever you're near a computer, right? (Answer: Well, no, you wouldn't, because they don't want to pay you for gazing at TikTok when they hired you to populate datasets.)

Colleges may not be paying you, but they want to see signs of diligence and motivation, just like employers do. Therefore, don't settle on topics or examples that indicate a lack of goals, a hatred of study, or a carelessness with one's work.

If you were applying for a job at IBM, you wouldn't talk about how excited you were to have an opportunity to work for Apple. That's not an easy mistake to make in person, but it *is* one that we've seen students make when submitting essays, especially when adapting one submission for multiple schools. Make sure you tailor your essay for the school you're actually submitting to!

**❷ Leave out any off-color or illegal material, or anything else that places you in a questionable light.**

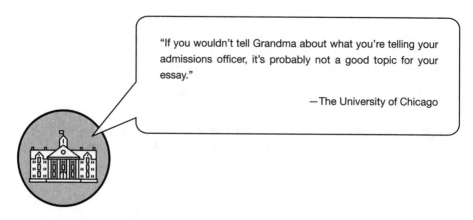

"If you wouldn't tell Grandma about what you're telling your admissions officer, it's probably not a good topic for your essay."

—The University of Chicago

**EXAMPLE:** Maybe you and some friends stole a street sign on junior prom night. It doesn't matter if that's a rite of passage in your high school or if it seems funny to you. Unless you're using this as an example of a valuable, life-changing lesson about *not* going along with the crowd, be careful how much you reveal in your essay. You'll probably want to stay away from anything illegal. (This goes for anything risqué or off-color, too).

Step back from your personal attachment to a story and look at it from an admissions officer's perspective. They don't want you taking their school's street signs or doing anything else illegal once you're on campus, right? It could give them pause, even if you were otherwise about to be an admit.

If you're unsure, ask a high school counselor or your English teacher to give feedback on topics or read the essay.

**❸ Think long and hard before using humor or creative approaches.**

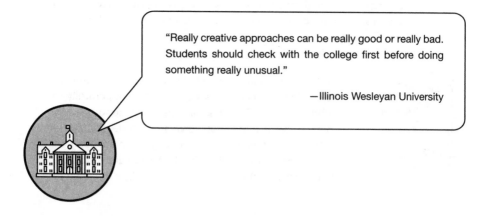

"Really creative approaches can be really good or really bad. Students should check with the college first before doing something really unusual."

—Illinois Wesleyan University

We'll get into this in more depth in Chapter 4, but in short, our insiders advise thinking very hard before including humor or overly creative approaches. Humor is very subjective; what's uproarious to one person (you) might make an admissions office take pause.

This holds true for essays including rhymes, limericks, and other non-standard forms. What reads as tremendously clever to you might cause an admissions officer to wonder if you're incapable of following directions.

It's a very good idea to get feedback from college counselors and teachers if you elect to choose one of these routes. If it meets with approval from these advisors, go for it. If not, take a different tack.

## ④ Beware of commonly used topics.

Admissions staff are bored by essays which show little effort or provide little insight into an applicant. Submitting a grammatically sound essay is a start but is insufficient. The applicant's task is to reveal something new about him or her that he could not be easily discerned from a list of curricular and co-curricular activities.

—Earlham University

Despite the massive number of applications most colleges receive every year, certain essay topics come up frequently. In the recent past, for example, essays on service trips, athletic injuries, and the death of a loved one (grandparent, parent) topped the list.

We've said this before, but it can't hurt to repeat it: Admissions staff work diligently to approach each essay with the care and thought it deserves. *But they are only human.* If yours is the third essay they read *in one day* on how coming back from an injury motivated you to pull through tough times, they may mentally sigh and be unable to muster enthusiasm.

That's why it's always best to find topics that are unique to you—stories that other applicants couldn't tell, or at least couldn't phrase the same way—and which would therefore help you to be memorable.

To be clear, this doesn't mean that you can't still write about breaking your leg in a soccer game. It just means that you'll need to work even harder to elevate this essay above the others that may be just like it. If specific, stand-out details about your chosen prompt don't come readily to mind, you may want to choose a less-trodden path to go down.

# END OF CHAPTER REVIEW

In this chapter, we've given you a look behind the Admissions Office curtain. We've shown you who reads your application, in what conditions, and what admissions officers look for. We've reviewed the systems that may be used to evaluate your application, discussed how much weight institutions place on essays and, finally, advised you about common torpedoes that can scuttle an essay.

You don't have to do this brainstorming now, but it's a good idea to at least start generating topics and ideas as you proceed.

**What story do you want to tell?**

_____

_____

_____

**What do you *not* want to share with this audience?**

_____

_____

_____

**How can you refocus the kernel of your essay *for* this particular audience?**

_____

_____

_____

# Chapter 2: Finding Your Perfect Topic

## How to Generate Engaging Ideas and Develop Your Unique Story

Are you a culinary whiz? An amateur genealogist? A spelunker? Each of these topics has the potential to be an excellent college essay that will keep your reader engaged and reveal who you are beyond the data and activities on your application. But that potential can be squandered if you shift topics mid-essay or fail to fully respond to the given prompt.

In this chapter, we'll:

- teach you how to break down a prompt so you can better stay on topic

- review a list of "tired" essay topics to avoid

- guide you through the process of writing a cohesive personal statement that also helps you stand out as an applicant

# CHOOSING A PROMPT

While the type of essay you'll have to submit may change from school to school, there are some basic guidelines that hold true. The following tips are modeled after samples found on the Common Application, which provides six specific, directed prompts to choose between, or a seventh that is open to the topic of your choice. It is your job to select the prompt that most inspires you to share your story, break it down into the questions posed in the prompt, and write an essay that is engaging and personal while responding to these questions.

The key here is to remember that your college essay is also referred to as your personal statement, so keep it *personal.*

There are two ways to approach the Common Application prompts: If you already have a topic in mind, keep narrowing down the prompts until you find the one that best suits your topic. If you don't already have an idea, look to the prompts. Find the one that speaks to you, the one that you feel inspired to write about.

Inspiration is important because this is the only part of the application that you have *complete* control over. Everything else is "fill in the blanks" data. This is your chance not only to share a compelling story, but to *tell it* so compellingly that your reader can almost see you and hear your voice.

# Sample Prompts from the 2020–2021 Common Application

Each of these prompts has a word count requirement that's between 250–650 words, and there's no one prompt that a college is looking for *more* than any other. All things being equal, choose the one that's most useful to *you*.

**❶** Some students have a background, identity, interest, or talent so meaningful they believe their application would be incomplete without it. If this sounds like you, please share your story.

**❷** The lessons we take from obstacles we encounter can be fundamental to later success. Recount a time when you faced a challenge, setback, or failure. How did it affect you and what did you learn from the experience?

**❸** Reflect on a time when you questioned or challenged a belief or idea. What prompted your thinking? What was the outcome?

**❹** Describe a problem you've solved or a problem you'd like to solve. It can be an intellectual challenge, a research query, an ethical dilemma—anything of personal importance, no matter the scale. Explain its significance to you and what steps you took or could be taken to identify the solution.

**❺** Discuss an accomplishment, event, or realization that sparked a period of personal growth and a new understanding of yourself or others.

**❻** Describe a topic, idea, or concept you find so engaging it makes you lose all track of time. Why does it captivate you? What or who do you turn to when you want to learn more?

**❼** Share an essay on any topic of your choice. It can be one you've already written, one that responds to a different prompt, or one of your own design.

## ACTIVITY

Whether or not you're ready to write your essay, just put down your initial feelings about these prompts right now. List the numbers of each prompt on the scale below according to how prepared you feel to write about it.

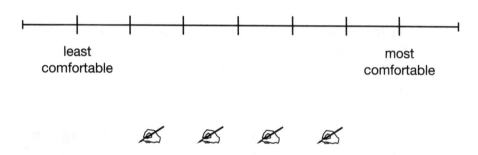

least
comfortable

most
comfortable

# BREAKING DOWN A PROMPT

For the most part, each prompt includes two to four questions, each of which must be fully answered. To make sure you stay on topic, break the prompt down into its separate components and respond to each question. Literally.

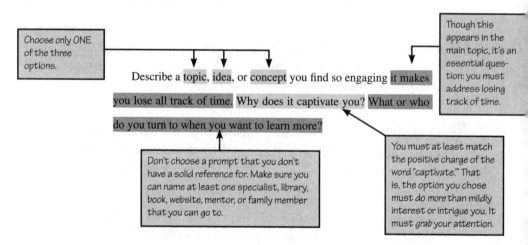

Choose only ONE of the three options.

Though this appears in the main topic, it's an essential question: you must address losing track of time.

Describe a topic, idea, or concept you find so engaging it makes you lose all track of time. Why does it captivate you? What or who do you turn to when you want to learn more?

Don't choose a prompt that you don't have a solid reference for. Make sure you can name at least one specialist, library, book, website, mentor, or family member that you can go to.

You must at least match the positive charge of the word "captivate." That is, the option you chose must do more than mildly interest or intrigue you. It must grab your attention.

# ACTIVITY

Once you've broken down the prompt, start brainstorming options for your topic. Don't overthink it; just write a list of whatever comes to your mind. This is a pre-write to provide ideas for you to choose from. Below, we've demonstrated the sort of brainstorming we did on a specific topic for each prompt. Follow along and give yourself a few minutes to do your own brainstorming (on your own topic).

> ### Describe a topic, idea, or concept you find so engaging it makes you lose all track of time. Why does it captivate you? What or who do you turn to when you want to learn more?

**Our brainstorming:**

- physics
- eating
- dwarf stars
- cooking
- genealogy
- sleeping
- reading
- watching YouTube
- watching TED talks
- crafting
- gaming
- coding

**Your brainstorming:**

_____

_____

_____

_____

_____

_____

_____

_____

_____

_____

_____

_____

Though you'll only ultimately choose to write about one topic, idea, or concept, when you're brainstorming, don't set limits. You may have a concept in mind, but when you review the list you've written, you may realize that there's a more compelling idea.

Avoid tired, overused topics that your reader has seen hundreds of times. (Later in the chapter we provide a list of cliché topics and an exercise for you to identify weak essay ideas.) Be unique! Your topic should be both personal and compelling.

"Tell your story, allow yourself to think and feel freely when writing, and enjoy the process of self-discovery."

—University of Richmond

Because the remaining parts of this question rely upon the topic, idea, or concept you've chosen here, you should choose one before continuing. If you run into trouble brainstorming because of the topic you chose, try selecting a new one. We've chosen genealogy.

Describe a topic, idea, or concept you find so engaging it **makes you lose all track of time.** Why does it captivate you? What or who do you turn to when you want to learn more?

**Our brainstorming:**

- I went to the library before lunch and suddenly the librarian tapped me on the shoulder to tell me they were closing. Six hours passed in no time!

- My parents sometimes forget I'm home when I'm at my computer following a long-lost relative's trail.

- I go to the Mormon Temple archives almost every Saturday to use their amazing database. I arrive at nine in the morning, when they open, and before I know it, four hours have passed, my stomach is growling with hunger and I have to eat lunch. After lunch, I return to the archives and get lost in my research until the lights flash, telling me it's closing time.

**Your brainstorming:**

_____

_____

_____

_____

_____

_____

_____

_____

_____

_____

_____

You don't need to fully develop each example of how you've lost track of time, but you do need to write specifically enough so that when you come back to develop your essay, your notes are clear. If you simply say that your parents forget you're at home when you're at your computer, how does that connect to your topic?

"[I love to see] anything that reveals a personality."

—DePaul University

Describe a topic, idea, or concept you find so engaging it makes you lose all track of time. **Why does it captivate you?** What or who do you turn to when you want to learn more?

**Potential brainstorming:**

- I am an only child who has yearned for an expanded family ever since I can remember.

- I feel connected to the life stories of relatives relatives who died long before I was born.

- I learned that I'm related to Jean Lafitte, the pirate!

- My DNA test showed that my family originated in France, not Ireland. We always thought we were pure Irish!

- I'm now known as the family genealogist! Relatives email me with hints and questions about lost family members.

- I can't believe that a single swab in my cheek opened an entire world to me that I did not know existed. I now feel connected to hundreds of people I've never met.

**Your brainstorming:**

_____

_____

_____

_____

_____

_____

_____

_____

_____

_____

_____

_____

The emphasis in this sliver is on "you." This is where brainstorming can really free you, as you shouldn't be thinking about what others might think or want. Right now, only write down the things you care about.

Assuming that an essay is well presented then what admissions staff loves to see is originality, or an authentic voice... [Has the reader] learned something new or interesting about the writer? Has the reader been informed, engaged in reflection or, for example, compelled to laugh?

—Earlham College

Describe a topic, idea, or concept you find so engaging it makes you lose all track of time. Why does it captivate you? What or who do you turn to when you want to learn more?

**Potential brainstorming:**

- The Mormon Temple in my hometown, Los Angeles, holds one of the most comprehensive genealogy records in the world. I spend hours there every weekend. The historians are so knowledgeable and always take time to send me in a new direction when I'm stuck in a search.

- I talk to my grandparents and write down their stories about relatives.

- I use two genealogy websites where I sent my DNA to find extended family and learn about family history. Every time I open a site, I have hints and messages waiting for me. I've communicated with many relatives on these sites.

- A cousin who is also working on our family tree.

**Your brainstorming:**

_____

_____

_____

_____

_____

_____

_____

_____

_____

_____

_____

Remember that these are not standalone questions, but interconnected ones. As you brainstorm people that you turn to, make sure you're specifically listing the ones who can help you learn more about your chosen topic. Note how our examples speak to people who can help with genealogy.

"A lot of students think that they have to cure cancer or do some extraordinary event [for it to be a good essay]. The simple thing can be just as rewarding and give you as much of a learning experience."

—St. Mary's College of Maryland

# ACTIVITY

## Making Effective Choices

Select one of the five remaining prompts that most speaks to you and take a shot at your own brainstorming. Because you're just pre-writing at this point, it's okay to write down things that you'll later discard. Also, don't feel obligated to try and stretch a prompt into four parts—you might choose one that has fewer than four. This breakdown is designed to help you write the full essay later, so use however much you find helpful. Just remember to answer the entire question.

**Prompt # ___:** _____

_____

_____

**Part 1:**

_____

_____

_____

**Part 2:**

_____

_____

_____

**Part 3:**

_____

_____

_____

**Part 4:**

_____

_____

_____

# CHOOSING YOUR TOPIC

Avoid writing about a tired, overused topic. Here are a few examples of topics that have become cliché from overuse:

- I scored the winning point (touchdown, basket, home run, goal).

- My fight against a disease (like fundraising for a cure for cancer).

- I moved to the United States when I was six and didn't speak English.

- I went to a foreign country on a community service trip.

- It's really hard to get good grades.

- A person (usually a close relative) means everything to me.

"I would like to see more students write about their personal feelings and journey. Essays focusing on athletics, the passing of a loved one, or their favorite TV show often does not convey the nature or personality of the applicant."

—Moravian College

# ACTIVITY

## Topics That Spark Joy

Here's a list of topics. Cross out the ones you think are too commonly used, inappropriate, or vague.

- the challenge of college applications
- my favorite pet
- how I learned to collaborate in my internship
- why I didn't make the team
- my family's annual trips
- publishing my first book
- learning to cook
- why I should be class president
- my summer at NASA
- training service dogs

- learning beyond the classroom
- a recap of my accomplishments
- what I learned from my autistic brother
- my most difficult class
- why my community is narrow minded
- I've lived in six countries and seven states
- I don't believe it's almost senior year
- when my best friend moved away
- my research in a biomedical engineering lab
- learning about customer service at work

Look at the remaining topics. Circle two or three that you find exciting. What is it about these that thrills you?

_____

_____

_____

There is an overarching topic that we suggest students avoid mentioning in ANY essay: mental health issues. While your admissions reader may feel empathy when learning about your depression, anxiety, eating disorder, or any other psychological challenge, colleges are risk averse! Consciously or not, readers may view your application less favorably as a result of this revelation, questioning whether their school would be the best fit for your needs, or wondering whether the stressors of their program might be too much. That should be a decision for *you* and you alone to make when considering whether to attend a school that has accepted you, so while you should absolutely *not* be ashamed of this sort of personal struggle, you may want to keep it out of your essay.

# SETTING UP AN INTRODUCTION

Think about the first lines of novels that you've chosen to read all the way through. Look at some headlines that caught your attention. Consider which paragraphs in a magazine article kept you reading. None of those openings are accidental! They're carefully constructed to pull you in, which is especially important when there are thousands of other materials you could be reading instead.

College admissions officers *have* to read your essay, but they don't have to engage with it. Don't let them glaze right past you! Open with a solid hook that grabs their attention and inspires them not only to read more closely but to remember you.

What do the following first lines have in common?

- I was a finalist on *American* Idol.

- My favorite recipe has 35 ingredients.

- The stranger grabbed my backpack and jumped off the train.

- I published my first book when I was nine years old.

- My family is full of spies.

- A giraffe ate my baseball cap.

Your mileage may vary, but for the most part, aren't you the slightest bit curious about what comes next? Who are those mysterious spies? How can I publish a book?

## ACTIVITY

### Stranger than Fiction

First, just write three hooks. It doesn't matter if they're true or not. Just have them be something guaranteed to grab your reader's attention.

_____

_____

_____

Now, using the same principles, write two hooks that are based on actual events. Don't exaggerate or lie. Just find a surprising detail to focus on.

_____

_____

_____

"[I love to see] unique stories students have to offer that tell me something about themselves that I can't ascertain from their admission file."

—Hanover College

## SETTING UP THE STORY

The following is a sample essay based on the prompt we discussed earlier in the chapter. As you read, look to see how the writer answered each part of the prompt. Also pay close attention to lines that grab your attention.

The prompt has been reprinted here. You shouldn't include it at the top of your essay when you submit it, but you should keep it at the top of the page while you write so that you can keep checking back to be sure that you're not straying off topic.

**Prompt:** Describe a topic, idea, or concept you find so engaging it makes you lose all track of time. Why does it captivate you? What or who do you turn to when you want to learn more?

This story has a great hook that immediately catches the reader's attention.

The writer introduces his topic early in the essay.

My great, great, great, great, great uncle is the pirate Jean Lafitte! I am an amateur genealogist, and I learned this shocking fact when researching my family history. I was at the Mormon Temple, the best place for genealogical research in my hometown of Los Angeles, when I traced my connection to this scallywag. I was so shocked that I let out a shout of surprise, attracting the attention (and annoyance) of dozens of fellow researchers. I heard more than one "Shh!" hissed my way. My favorite historian, Ms. Sutton, put her finger to her lips as she approached me with a smile. "So, Tim, what inspired your outburst?" she whispered, crouching at my carrel. "Ms. Sutton," I stammered quietly, my face red with embarrassment, "I'm related to a pirate! Jean Lafitte!" Her blue eyes twinkled behind her glasses, "Ah, what a discovery! This news will be a fun surprise for your family." I nodded with excitement as she returned to her desk, and my eyes darted back to the screen, now filled with drawings and paintings of the pirate, typically wearing a big black hat adorned with a long white feather. "Wow, a pirate!" I said under my breath.

Dialog brings the reader into the story and makes them feel involved in the action.

This sentence responds to the prompt's point about losing track of time.

Immersed in one story after the next about my infamous relative, I was startled when the lights flashed, signaling the center was closing. "There's never enough time," I thought as I made my way out into the dusk. My mom honked her horn, something she insists on doing that drives me crazy, and I clumsily ran towards our black Volvo, burdened by my heavy backpack. I couldn't wait to tell her the news! She is my biggest fan and responsible for this fascination with my family tree. The DNA test kit she gave me for my 16th birthday got me started on this quest that eats up most of my free time and makes me feel like part of a massive community rather than an only child. "Guess what, Mom?" I blurted as I pitched my backpack on the floor. "What fun fact did you learn today, Tim?" She replied. "We're French, not

This statement is a sidebar that adds nothing to the essay and wastes valuable words.

Irish, and related to the pirate Jean Lafitte on Dad's side!" I felt a sense of pride as I shared this astounding fact with my mom. "Wait until Dad hears about this!" Then, I remembered my dad was gone for two weeks. He never calls home from business trips, so I'd have to wait to tell him the news.

This detail is not relevant to the story and distracts the reader.

Nothing compares to the feeling of astonishment I experienced when my DNA came back with hundreds of matches and near matches. As the only child of two busy attorneys, I spend more time alone or with friends than with my family. I've always wanted a sibling, but something happened, and my mom couldn't have any children after I was born. Now, I have a newfound sense of belonging in TWO families—my newfound DNA relatives and the dozens of friends I've made through my research. Many fellow genealogists are older than me, but we share a joy of history and a passion for family, as well as an occasional PB&J sandwich. My DNA data revealed that I have second cousins nearby and many other relatives on the East Coast.

This sentence is off topic and overly personal.

The writer skillfully and subtly introduces his intellectual strengths, which are sure to be noticed by admissions readers.

Another reason genealogy has hooked me (pun intended) is that it's a scavenger hunt that uses my skills of deduction and memory. My memory is my biggest asset when it comes to finding a relative. I can take two seemingly disparate facts and put them together to find someone else to add to the tree. My grandparents are a great help with dates. We've grown much closer since I started my research. Right now, most of these people are strangers, but I know that over time I'll meet more of my extended family. Maybe I'll organize a pirate-themed family reunion next summer! Arr!

The essay ends on an upbeat note and the final "sentence" connects back to the opening line.

A note about word count. In this context, the acceptable length of a personal statement is between 250 and 650 words. It is virtually impossible for a student to communicate anything insightful and personal in 250 words. Most writers end up trimming their essays down to the maximum count of 650. We feel that a personal statement with a word count that falls somewhere between 500 and 650 is a good length. As long as you hit every point in the prompt, don't try to stretch your essay to 650 words if you finish writing at 550. More is not always better.

The addition of dialog is an excellent way to keep a story fresh and dynamic. The reader shares information by telling another character about it rather than through traditional sentence structure. A word of warning: if you use dialog, triple check your punctuation.

# ACTIVITY

## Answering the Question(s)

Analyze this essay and underline where it answers (if it answers) each part of the prompt. Observe how subtly most of the information is inserted into the essay, and how it seamlessly flows into the story. Enter your responses below.

**Part 1: Describe a topic, idea, or concept you find so engaging ...**

_____

_____

**Part 2: ... it makes you lose all track of time.**

_____

_____

**Part 3: Why does it captivate you?**

_____

_____

**Part 4: What or who do you turn to when you want to learn more?**

_____

_____

# ACTIVITY

## Be Prompt About It!

See if you can match each opening line to its corresponding prompt. For extra practice, see if you can come up with a better opening.

| Prompt | Topic |
|---|---|
| 1. Some students have a background, identity, interest, or talent so meaningful they believe their application would be incomplete without it. If this sounds like you, please share your story. | A. My physics research project kept leading me to dead ends.<br><br>PROMPT: _____ |
| 2. The lessons we take from obstacles we encounter can be fundamental to later success. Recount a time when you faced a challenge, setback, or failure. How did it affect you and what did you learn from the experience? | B. I am fascinated by the work we can do to help babies survive in utero.<br><br>PROMPT: _____ |
| 3. Reflect on a time when you questioned or challenged a belief or idea. What prompted your thinking? What was the outcome? | C. When I was nine years old, I accidentally discovered that I was adopted.<br><br>PROMPT: _____ |
| 4. Describe a problem you've solved or a problem you'd like to solve. It can be an intellectual challenge, a research query, an ethical dilemma—anything of personal importance, no matter the scale. Explain its significance to you and what steps you took or could be taken to identify the solution. | D. I decided to stop attending church with my family in seventh grade.<br><br>PROMPT: _____ |
| 5. Discuss an accomplishment, event, or realization that sparked a period of personal growth and a new understanding of yourself or others. | E. I have lived in six countries and nine states.<br><br>PROMPT: _____ |

Some topics may be appropriate for more than one prompt. When brainstorming for your essay, it's up to you to determine which prompt best suits your topic, or vice versa. Select the option that most inspires you to write a story that communicates the essence of your personality.

The answers are A 2, B 4, C 5, D 3, and E 1.

# FINDING THE THEME IN A SUPPLEMENTAL ESSAY

So far, we've looked at the sort of personal statement that you're most likely going to be asked to submit through things like the Common Application. But depending on where you apply, you may also be asked to answer other types of questions. These will probe your interest in and knowledge of the school, so do your research and be specific!

Schools often release their topics to students by August 1. Be sure to check these as soon as they're available.

## What's the Same?

Where your personal statement is specific to you, these supplemental essay should be tailored to the school that has requested it. Note that you can and should still share information that makes you an impossible-to-ignore candidate; you must do so in a way that also highlights the institution where possible.

You should tackle the supplemental essay in the same way that you approached the personal statement. Break the question into however many parts you need to assure that you answer each part. Be particularly cautious here, as going off-topic will signal to the college that you didn't do your homework and aren't a serious candidate.

Even if two schools have similar prompts for their supplemental essays, be careful about recycling your responses. You'll often be asked to provide specific details, and there's nothing more embarrassing than realizing that you submitted an essay that mentioned a different college by name!

## What's Different?

Supplemental essays tend to be more focused on the following four common topics:

- Why this school?

- Why this major?

- What is your favorite activity?

- How is community important to you?

Supplemental essays are often packed with specific keywords and phrases that serve as hints about what the college wants you to focus on. Here are some common ones to look out for:

- In and outside the classroom
- How it has influenced you
- Depth and breadth
- Unique
- Collaborate
- Current and past experiences
- Talent or interest
- What role you play

# WHY THIS SCHOOL?

Here are some of the ways in which you may see this prompt.

- As you seek admission to the Class of 2024, what aspects of the College's program, community, or campus environment attract your interest?
- Please tell us what you value most about College X and why.
- What excites you about College X's intellectually playful community? In short, Why College X?

 ## Do

You *can* talk about the location, but only if there's a specific and compelling reason for doing so. For instance, if you're planning to major in politics, talk about the excellent internships and experiences available in the D.C. area. Even better, however, would be to discuss how the school's career center might be able to help you take advantage of those opportunities.

## Don't

These may seem simple enough to answer honestly, but that's the pitfall of this type of question. Don't give a simple, facile, or generic answer. These are the subjects to avoid discussing. (Remember, part of this comes down to how the school sees itself.)

- the college's elite reputation and high ranking
- how much money graduates earn
- how much you enjoyed the food on your campus visit
- the cute cafes and restaurants in the neighborhood
- the weather

# ACTIVITY

## Identify Your Deal Breakers

Either choose a college that you've already visited and researched or take the time now to gather some information from a prospective college's website. Jot down anything that seems particularly appealing to you. Avoid anything general. To help focus your search, list your top three deal-breaker questions, the things that you need any college to have, and make sure you get at least the answers to those.

Top Three Questions: _____

_____

_____

College Name: _____

Interesting Things: _____

Answer to Question 1: _____

Answer to Question 2: _____

Answer to Question 3: _____

# WHY THIS MAJOR?

As with all the supplemental topics, specificity is key. Note that, in addition to providing your motivation for learning a subject, many of these sample prompts are likely to ask how the school itself can help support you. Don't sleep on that part of the response! It is just as, if not more, important!

- Describe the unique qualities that attract you to the specific undergraduate college or school to which you are applying at College X. How would that curriculum support your interests?

- College X's Open Curriculum allows students to explore broadly while also diving deeply into their academic pursuits. Tell us about an academic interest (or interests) that excites you, and how you might use the Open Curriculum to pursue it.

- For applicants to College X, tell us what from your current and past experiences (either academic or personal) attracts you specifically to the field or fields of study that you noted in the Application Data section.

## 👍 Do

- YOUR reason for selecting a major is the most valid! Do not worry that a reader will judge you for your motivation in choosing an area of study.

- If your inspiration to study creative writing sprung from your mom reading you bedtime stories when you were a kid, then that's your reason.

- If you want to be an architect because you spent hours building your designs out of Lego bricks as a child, then that's your reason.

- If you're going to work in genetics because your grandfather has Alzheimer's and you want to advance knowledge in this area, then that's your reason.

## 👎 Don't

- You can discuss a career track, but the focus of the essay should be specifically on the degree that you plan on studying at the school you're applying to. For instance, "pre-med" is not a major, but rather a path to medical school.

- Since most pre-med students are biology or chemistry majors, the better choice is for you to discuss the specific subject area you want to study and how that will prepare you for medical school.

- The emphasis must be on your undergraduate degree.

# What if You're "Undeclared"?

Don't worry. Not every sixteen or seventeen year old has their future planned. You can put a spin on this question by writing that you are going to college to learn about your career options and will dive into a variety of studies until you find your calling. Mention a few areas of study you look forward to exploring. With few exceptions, you don't have to declare a major until the end of your second year of college, so you have time to explore your options. Many students switch their concentration a few times before finalizing their degree choice. Even then, most of us have multiple careers throughout our lives.

Beware of subtle differences in majors from school to school. For example, one college may offer an Environmental Science major, where the same major is called Earth Science at another school. Admissions readers catch these mistakes, and they do not reflect well on your application.

# ACTIVITY
## Bite-Sized Pieces

Choose one of the three sample prompts for the "Why this Major" question (page 56) and break it down into as many pieces as necessary. Brainstorm how you might respond to each.

**Prompt # ___:** _____

_____

_____

**Part 1:**

_____

_____

_____

**Part 2:**

_____

_____

_____

**Part 3:**

_____

_____

_____

**Part 4:**

_____

_____

_____

# WHAT IS YOUR FAVORITE ACTIVITY?

With only 150–250 words allotted for this subject, it's important that you make every word count. This can be a blessing and a curse. It should be easy and fun to write about something that you know and love and regularly do. At the same time, it can be hard to limit yourself and to stay on topic when you just want to gush. To help focus, be sure that you choose only _one_ favorite pursuit, and for maximum effect, try to select one that relates to your major, especially if you're entering a focused area of study like engineering, film, drama, architecture, or computer science.

**Option 1:** If you could only do one of the activities you have listed in the Activities section of your Common Application, which one would you keep doing? Why?

**Option 2:** Please briefly elaborate on one of your extracurricular activities or work experiences.

Note that this supplemental essay might also ask even more specifically about a scholastic field as opposed to an activity of your choice.

**Option 3:** Describe your favorite academic subject and explain how it has influenced you.

## 👍 Do

- Use meaningful, personal language rather than generic terms. This is a personal essay about your favorite activity and should include specific details about the pursuit and why it excites you. This writing style should communicate your enthusiasm for the topic.

- Be specific. This essay is not a global "save the world" or "cure cancer" response. If your favorite extracurricular involves cancer research, elaborate on why you enjoy the process rather than focusing on the overall research goal.

- Read the prompt carefully and pay attention to the keywords that direct your essay into a specific topic or direction.

## Don't

- Repeat a topic included in another essay or your personal statement.

- Brag. Do not try to impress admissions readers with your accomplishments. Be sincere and write an essay about YOUR favorite activity, not the activity or award that you think admissions wants to read about.

# ACTIVITY

## Fill In the Blanks

Fill in the blanks of this sample activity essay with words and phrases that express a real or made-up activity. The goal here is to be enthusiastic.

I can't imagine a day without _____. My first attempt at

_____ was _____, and I haven't stopped for the

past _____. When I _____ my early efforts _____

_____, _____! I thought I

would be the next _____, but I _____.

Over the years, I _____ and _____

in both _____. I was excited to receive my fist

_____ to _____recently!

Here's an example of how you might fill out this type of essay. Obviously, you wouldn't just be filling in the blanks with yours, but this should give you an idea of the overall tone and level of detail to include.

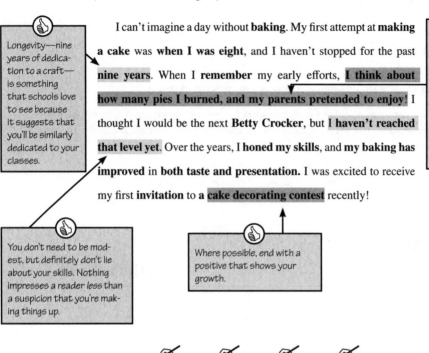

I can't imagine a day without **baking**. My first attempt at **making a cake** was **when I was eight**, and I haven't stopped for the past **nine years**. When I **remember** my early efforts, **I think about how many pies I burned, and my parents pretended to enjoy!** I thought I would be the next **Betty Crocker**, but **I haven't reached that level yet**. Over the years, I **honed my skills**, and **my baking has improved** in **both taste and presentation.** I was excited to receive my first **invitation** to a **cake decorating contest** recently!

Longevity—nine years of dedication to a craft—is something that schools love to see because it suggests that you'll be similarly dedicated to your classes.

Specifics are good, but especially details that convey something positive about you. In this case, a reader can see that you didn't let mistakes stop you.

You don't need to be modest, but definitely don't lie about your skills. Nothing impresses a reader less than a suspicion that you're making things up.

Where possible, end with a positive that shows your growth.

# HOW IS COMMUNITY IMPORTANT TO YOU?

Don't be thrown off by the use of the word "community." When you enroll in a college, you will be joining *their* community, and this question is mainly used to get a sense of how well you have previously fit in with groups (and whether you'll be involved on campus). This type of prompt also gives you another great opportunity to reveal something about yourself, namely, what makes you feel at home.

**Prompt 1.** Everyone belongs to many different communities or groups defined by (among other things) shared geography, religion, ethnicity, income, cuisine, interest, race, ideology, or intellectual heritage. Choose one of the communities to which you belong and describe that community and your place within it.

**Prompt 2.** Tell us about a place or community you call home. How has it shaped your perspective?

# 👍 Do

- Keep an open mind about the definition of a community. ANY group you belong to is a community.

- Use this essay to explain a new aspect of who you are and what you do so the admissions reader learns more about your personality.

- Feel free to elaborate on something from your activity list. Here is your opportunity to expand your explanation of a key group activity that you want to share with admissions. You can use the **group** as your community.

# 👎 Don't

- Address potentially controversial topics in your community essay. For example, if you are an avid hunter and belong to a community of hunters, choose another community. Why? Because you do not know how your reader feels about hunting or about guns.

- Overlook a multi-part prompt. This question asks about a community you call home AND how it has shaped your perspective. You will fail to follow directions if you overlook any part of the prompt!

A community can be any number of people that have gathered together in support of a certain thing. They can be large groups formed around neighborhoods, backgrounds, and beliefs, common shared interests and activities, or niche groups and clubs. Here are just a few types of communities that are acceptable topics for this prompt, as well as some of their subgroups.

Readers

- By genre
- By book club

Athletics

- Players
- Boosters
- Specific sports

Gamers

- eSports enthusiasts
- Dungeons and Dragons groups
- Massively Multiplayer Online Role-Playing clans

Religions

- By faith

- By outreach groups

School Communities

- Student Government

- National Honor Societies

- Clubs and other extracurriculars

The list goes on and on—you could be in a community of crafters, musicians, cooks, researchers, activists, and more. Your family even counts. Just be sure that whichever community you choose is one that satisfies the definition of the prompt and which will allow you to answer all parts of the question.

# ACTIVITY

List five communities you belong to:

1. _____

2. _____

3. _____

4. _____

5. _____


**Which community is your favorite, and why?** _____

_____

_____

_____

# END OF CHAPTER REVIEW

Phew! At this point, your brain is probably swimming with essay topics and you may be a bit overwhelmed. In this chapter we have shown you how to break down prompts, points to strive for and topics to avoid, and given you a preview of the prompts for your personal statement and supplemental essays. That's a TON of information to digest! Don't worry, you will relax once you start writing. As with many challenging things in our lives, the hardest part is getting started. So, let's get started!

Write the first thing that comes to mind for the following questions. Don't overthink!

**What is your dream college?**_____

**What is your major/potential major?**_____

**What is your favorite activity?** _____

**What community are you most involved in?** _____

See how easy it is to get started by answering a series of simple questions? Now turn on that computer or grab a pad of paper and a pen and start writing!

# Chapter 3: Developing Your Essay

## How to Make Sure You've Got a Beginning, Middle, and End

By the time you apply to college, you will have a fully fleshed out personal statement, somewhere in the ballpark of 650 words. Right now, however, you're likely only sitting on a pile of ideas and experiences and need to find a way to use them to showcase your uniqueness. In the previous chapter, you may have generated some eye-catching introductions, but now it's time to fill the page and no longer be intimidated by a blinking cursor or a blank screen.

In this chapter we'll:

- do some free-writing and brainstorming to overcome any blocks

- make sure your thesis provides as solid a foundation as possible for the rest of your essay

- plan out next steps using an outline

- look at various types of introductions

This chapter is designed to help develop your ideas, build your confidence, and give you the tools you need to:

- **begin** your essay

- **complete** a rough draft of your essay

- **stand out** from the other essays

# YOU AND THE BLANK SCREEN

The hardest part of writing is starting. Self-doubt lurks in the emptiness, filling your mind with questions like "Is having a strong essay topic good enough?" and "What's the best way to tell this story?" The only way to get past these questions is to trust in the process and start writing. You can always go back and revise once you're done, but the truth is that we all have to start somewhere, and that somewhere is a blank page.

If you find yourself really struggling, you may start considering schools that don't require you to write an essay. Resist this urge! You can still apply to those schools, but don't allow a surmountable obstacle like a personal statement to limit your choices. Apply where you *want* to apply, not to where you wind up *having* to apply.

## Setting Boundaries

Choosing an essay prompt is more helpful than you might as first think. It provides some basic guidelines as to what you should write about, ensuring that you don't just end up writing "I hate this" 216 times (however cathartic that might feel). Not having *any* topic leaves that page as empty as it will ever be. Choosing the topic of your college essay at the very least provides you with a task.

Putting together a rough draft, which is your next step, will help you even further in this regard. Think of this as assembling the ingredients for cooking or gathering a block of clay for sculpting. You may not necessarily use all the food you've chosen; you might reshape your clay several times, but you'll at least have narrowed down what you're working with. Each subsequent step will help you refine your choices.

The key is to not overwhelm yourself. You don't have to get it perfect on your first try. Forget perfect! Your rough draft doesn't even have to be in *good* shape! It just needs to be enough to get you started, so you're not drawing blanks.

You're going to be doing a lot of idea-generating writing in this chapter, and not just where you're prompted to fill in the blanks. So that you don't have to keep flipping between pages, put together a physical or computer folder where you can easily find all of your different exercises. Draw upon this as you work not only through this book but as you continue to polish your essay in your own time.

## Using Tools

Even the strongest writer doesn't simply conjure words out of thin air. Every writer, regardless of skill, uses certain tools to translate thoughts into written words. It won't surprise you, then, to learn that the more tools you bring to a writing assignment, the less difficult it will be to get started. (Try cutting a tomato without a knife.)

What may surprise you is that you're on more of an equal footing with your peers than you might think. Writing a college essay is a different exercise than any writing assignment you have ever done. Though a good essay will borrow many techniques from creative writing—it should be engaging, enjoyable, and surprising, like the best fiction—it's an entirely different project. However, knowing the fundamentals of proper grammar, the mechanics for connecting ideas, and having an overarching theme *will* help.

Don't get too creative with your interpretation of a topic. Poems, short stories, and screenplays do not make good college admission essays—emphasis on *essay.*

## Remove Distractions

Before you start writing, set yourself up for success. Make sure your chair is comfortable, your desk is clear of anything non-essay related, and put your phone somewhere that you can't see or hear it. Consider disconnecting your computer from the Internet or just use paper and pencil. (Some find the act of physically writing, as opposed to typing, to more fully engage the mind and body.) If you're in a public space and have access to noise-cancelling headphones, use them. If you're at home, ask your family not to disturb you.

Once you've set up your space, get your mind in the game. If you know any exercises to help you focus, run through them. Here are a few you might try:

- Sit still and count your breaths backward from twenty.

- Spend a few minutes visualizing something relaxing, like ocean waves or a gentle rainfall.

- Stretch your fingers, hands, forearms, arms, and shoulders.

# STEP 1: THE FREE WRITE

No matter how much planning you do, eventually, you just have to start writing. So pick some sort of topic, ideally one that's related to the prompt you want your personal statement to address. Set a timer somewhere from five to twenty minutes—we recommend starting at the lower end unless you already do this often. Turn off your internal editor and just write, putting whatever words come to mind on the page. When you're done, turn that editor back on and mark up your page. Highlight or circle anything that works. Cross out anything that doesn't. Repeat this process until you have enough material for a rough draft—and by "enough material" we mean two or three times as much as what you'll want for your final draft.

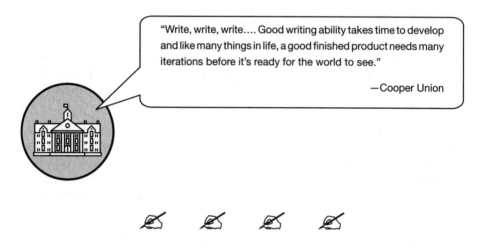

> "Write, write, write…. Good writing ability takes time to develop and like many things in life, a good finished product needs many iterations before it's ready for the world to see."
>
> —Cooper Union

## ACTIVITY

### Getting Started

If you don't yet have an essay topic or specific prompt in mind, try the ones below. These come directly from things college admissions counselors say they want to learn from reading a personal statement. Give yourself three minutes for each, writing as much as you can. When you do choose a topic, consider picking the one that most closely aligns with the one you have most easily and readily generated material for.

1. **What is your passion? How did you find it? What has it taught or given you?**

2. Describe a challenge you overcame. When did you show grit, courage, or persistence?

3. How do you see yourself? How do you see yourself growing in college?

4. What college are you the most excited about? Why?

5. Describe a time you experienced failure. How did you respond?

6. How would you describe your worldview? When have you had your point of view challenged?

# Fending off Writer's Block

Take a moment to think of your favorite three writers. Guess what? All three have probably experienced writer's block before! If you find yourself suffering from it, just remember that you're in good company, and that it doesn't at all reflect badly on you. What matters is what you do *next* to get past this block.

## ❶ Break your routine.

If you're stuck in a writing rut, break it. Get up from your chair. Grab a snack, go for a walk, take your mind away from the work. Don't treat this as an escape, though. It's not an excuse to start binging television or to avoid the work. Set a timer so you know when to get back to writing.

## ❷ Leave yourself hanging.

Think about how cliffhangers work on television or in books. They have you actively anticipating the next episode or chapter, ready to dive back in for more. You can also do this with your writing. Instead of exhausting every idea at once, end a session on an unfinished thought that you're excited to write about. Then, when you pick things back up, you'll already be ready to go.

## ❸ Jump around.

This isn't geometry. The shortest distance between two points doesn't have to be a straight line. If you're getting stuck on your introduction, jump to one of your paragraphs. If the conclusion is giving you grief, work on a different section.

## ❹ Talk it through.

If you can't bring yourself to pick up a pen, try recording yourself. Call up a friend or talk to a parent about what you're trying to do. Sometimes this can be enough to shake loose what you are trying to convey, or it might give you an idea for a new approach.

# STEP 2: THE THESIS

Ever gone bowling before? Now that you've successfully got the ball rolling, it's time to make sure you're aiming it correctly. To do so, you'll want to make sure that both you and your readers have a clear vision of your main idea. In argumentative or analytical writing, this is called your thesis statement.

Another way to look at your thesis is as a so-called "elevator pitch." How, in one or two sentences, would you persuade an admissions counselor that you're an excellent student to have on campus? Start there, and have the rest of your personal statement back up your thesis or pitch.

Your thesis is a clear characterization of the overall essay you're writing. These are two main ways to present it. One method is to put it in your introductory paragraph, which works when you're going to spend the rest of the essay backing up that claim. Another is to put it in your conclusion, which is effective if you've been describing a change throughout your essay. In either case, you'll need to have *some* version of your thesis in both the introduction and conclusion, and you'll want to make sure that each body paragraph clearly connects to it.

"Edit your essay carefully. Don't use big vocabulary words for the sake of puffing up your writing—it's clear that's what you're trying to do."

—College of the Atlantic

# ACTIVITY

## Building a Thesis Statement

Your goal here is to draft a rough thesis statement that emphasizes what you want a college admissions counselor to *most* learn about you in the essay. Imagine that you're constructing the building below: from the key qualities on the left and right, you'll fill out details in the middle, and then use those to complete the top floor--your overarching thesis. First fill in your key qualities, then choose two to list examples for in the middle, then take any common or unifying thought about those to write your thesis at the top.

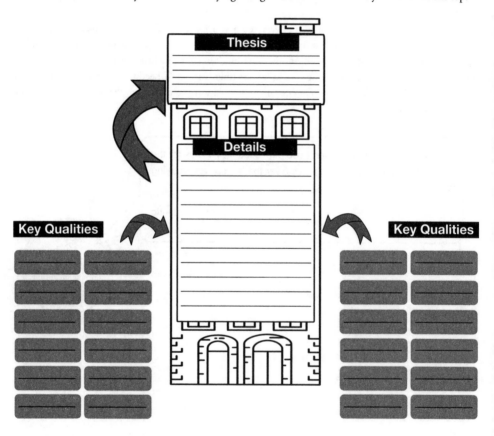

# STEP THREE: THE OUTLINE

Like other essays, personal statements use body paragraphs to develop and support the thesis. Body paragraphs can look different from one essay to another, but many will include elements you're familiar with from analytical writing: a topic sentence, evidence, and analysis. If you're stuck, use a description of yourself as the topic sentence, a personal experience as evidence, and a reflection on that experience as analysis.

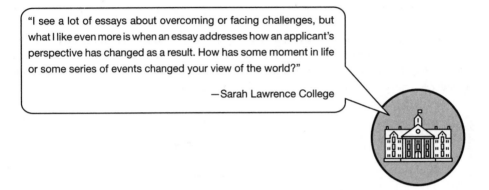

"I see a lot of essays about overcoming or facing challenges, but what I like even more is when an essay addresses how an applicant's perspective has changed as a result. How has some moment in life or some series of events changed your view of the world?"

—Sarah Lawrence College

These paragraphs might be organized by character traits you want to describe. Or, they could be organized chronologically if you're telling a story. Here's an example of how you might approach writing an essay about an experience that changed your life.

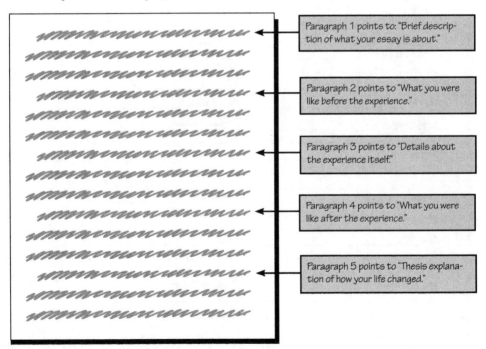

Paragraph 1 points to: "Brief description of what your essay is about."

Paragraph 2 points to "What you were like before the experience."

Paragraph 3 points to "Details about the experience itself."

Paragraph 4 points to "What you were like after the experience."

Paragraph 5 points to "Thesis explanation of how your life changed."

As you can see, we're not worried right now about what each paragraph specifically states. But by laying out a structure like this, we now have an outline for how to approach and make the most of each paragraph. That's the goal of outlining: to get the tough work of figuring out what you need to say out of the way. Now, when you write your essay, all you have to focus on is *how* to say it.

# ACTIVITY

## Develop Your Outline

Stories have a beginning, middle, and an end. You may deviate from such a straightforward presentation with your final draft, but for now, work on organizing your thoughts in that fashion. In the left-hand column, pick a favorite book and a favorite movie and break them down. Then, following the same principle, develop two of the topics you're thinking of using in the right-hand column.

**BOOK:** _____

Overall theme: _____

Beginning: _____

Middle: _____

End: _____

Lesson learned: _____

**MOVIE:** _____

Overall theme: _____

Beginning: _____

Middle: _____

End: _____

Lesson learned: _____

**TOPIC #1:** _____

Overall theme: _____

Beginning: _____

Middle: _____

End: _____

Lesson learned: _____

**TOPIC #2:** _____

Overall theme: _____

Beginning: _____

Middle: _____

End: _____

Lesson learned: _____

# STEP 4: BODY PARAGRAPHS AND CONCLUSION

If you've taken a road trip, you know that it's a good idea to start with some sort of map or route guidance. The work you've done to this point has essentially been assembling those directions. If you don't yet feel that you have enough rough, free-written material on your topic, and you're still shaky on your thesis and outline, take some time here to generate some more. When you're ready, let's put the car in gear and start developing those ideas into complete paragraphs.

Most introductions tend to pull from and describe what's been done in the body paragraphs, so for now, we recommend skipping it and coming back to it later.

## The Journey

Though we mentioned a road trip earlier, be aware that you do not have to write your essay from beginning to end. That said, you also don't want to get bogged down in detours. Find the compromise between the straight line and curved path that works for you, and use that outline to help stay on track as you twist and turn, write and rewrite, and remix all of your ideas into a final draft.

Whatever your route, your first step should probably be to use your outline to organize everything you've already written. Index cards of your ideas can be helpful here, as can copying and pasting if you're working digitally. As you add each piece, check it against your thesis, and leave notes about sections that need more development. Once you've collected everything, check to make sure that you have specific examples and that you're not repeating yourself. Make sure that you have specific examples and that you're not repeating yourself. Get the point?

"We love to see stories that back up the attributes they claim about themselves. If they say they are courageous, an example of how that was lived out is fantastic."

—Grove City College

# The Three Elements of a Personal Statement

There are three key elements in narrative non-fiction, the genre in which your essay belongs. Knowing these and using them will help you support your main ideas, make your writing clear and readable, and give you room to use creative writing for dramatic effect.

## ❶ Summary

Summaries are used to efficiently describe many things and to make connections between various points. They are the broad strokes of writing that serve to introduce further information. For instance, "In tenth grade, I was on the swim team, the debate team, and the school newspaper" or "I was a shy and nervous first-year when...."

## ❷ Detail

Often following from summaries, details are the specifics about a situation. These serve to explain and develop a topic, and often rely upon figurative language or imagery that engages the senses. For instance, "Debates were my sport of choice; I would spend all day dribbling ideas down my mind's court, taking shots with various points and counterpoints, and setting up rebuttals to block opponents with."

## ❸ Reflection

Reflections are like summaries, but instead of introducing more details, they often serve to encapsulate those that have already been presented. They're an opportunity to showcase yourself and the impact events have had on you, and they are a critical part of connecting the story that you're sharing to the topic required by a college. For instance, "It was through debate that I was able to build up the confidence necessary to start speaking my mind in class."

"[I remember an essay] about rutabagas—it was poetic, beautifully descriptive (lots of strong written images), personally meaningful, and intellectually sophisticated. It showed us who the applicant was: a glimpse of her life, her interests, the work she envisions herself doing in the world and in her community, and some of her incredible writing talent and potential. It was powerful, mature writing from a young person who had already developed a strong and compelling voice."

—College of the Atlantic

Here's an example of a successful body paragraph that braids together these three elements of writing.

Details are often tied to senses, in this case to a specific smell.

The so-called "rule of threes" suggests that we feel most comfortable with a set of three details, which is why we've gone from smell to taste to touch.

Looking back, I can still smell the six-molar ammonia when Dr. Warren stayed after school for two extra hours just so we could finish up our AP Chemistry labs. I can still taste the donuts that Mr. Tomlin bought those Saturday mornings when he drove us to middle school Academic Bowl tournaments. And I can still recall those warm afternoons when my kindergarten teacher, Mrs. Osteen, randomly stopped by my house just to say "hi." Such are the teachers who have shaped my character these past twelve years in school, and such are the teachers who build the foundations of our communities, guiding the paths of those who become our divas and CEOs. Such are the teachers who are my heroes.

Note how this second detail not only showcases a new sense, taste, but also ties back to the first, which also dealt with a teacher.

A summary doesn't always have to be at the start of a paragraph.

Note how the reflection connects vivid details and a summary to a purpose. The thesis in this example is likely dealing with a personal hero.

## ACTIVITY

### Put It to the Test: Part One

We've done a lot of abstract exercises so far, where you could write about anything. So here, let's try writing specifically about what you've *just* been doing in this chapter.

**Summarize** what you've worked on so far.

_____

_____

_____

List **details** about what you've done.

_____

_____

_____

Provide an **evocative** example of two of those details: be **creative**.

_____

_____

_____

**Reflect** on how this is going to help you.

_____

_____

_____

Now use the same techniques to build out the body paragraphs of your own essay. Keep everything organized so that you can find it later!

"[You can take] any theme—even a perfectly mundane one— and use it to illustrate a personal insight, thought process, or bigger idea that delves beneath the surface."

—College of the Atlantic

# STEP 5: THE CONCLUSION

One way to think of your conclusion is as a reflection or summary of your entire essay so far. This is where you'll want to reiterate the most important ideas and to really make sure that you've answered the topic question you chose. Remember, it's not just a matter of whether *you* understand how your facts relate to the question, but whether the admissions counselors will get it. This is especially important because while you may have written these sections out of order, this is the last thing a reader will be seeing.

Note: this is not the place to introduce new concepts or ideas. This is the home stretch of your journey—the act of parking the car after that road trip. All of the good work you've done to this point risks collapsing if you crash here!

If your essay is being submitted to a specific school, the phrase "bring it home" is particularly relevant here. Take the opportunity to address the institution itself, making it a part of the conclusion of your story. Don't try this if you're submitting an essay to multiple colleges at once, as with the Common Application.

## ACTIVITY

Now that you've had a chance to draft ideas for your body paragraphs (page 78), use this space to draft a conclusion.

_____

_____

_____

_____

_____

_____

Next, write the prompt that you based your body paragraphs on.

_____

_____

Draw a line from each question in the prompt to its answer in the conclusion. If you can't make a connection, draw that line to the side of the page and write down what's missing from the conclusion.

# STEP 6: THE INTRODUCTION

At long last, with a working draft of your thesis, body paragraphs, and conclusion on the once-blank page, it's time to turn back to the introduction. We've waited until now so that you could be as prepared as possible, because the introduction carries a lot of weight on its shoulders. It must:

- capture the reader's attention and interest

- clearly lead into your thesis

- uniquely stand apart from other essays

Don't be surprised if you find yourself returning to your opening lines over and over again. You'll be tinkering with them until they're just right.

# Make a Splash

One way to capture the reader's attention is to start big, by which we mean open with your Big Idea. This allows admissions counselors to immediately get a sense of your unique worldview, using your personality and sense of style to introduce the topic.

Think of an upside-down triangle. The point at the bottom represents your thesis: It is a specific statement that addresses the prompt directly or describes who you are as a college applicant. The side of the triangle at the top represents a Big Idea that begins your essay.

If you're skeptical of starting with a Big Idea, just look at the works of some great authors.

| Opening Line | Why it Works |
| --- | --- |
| "It is a truth universally acknowledged, that a single man in possession of a good fortune, must be in want of a wife." (*Pride and Prejudice*) | *Pride and Prejudice* centers around five sisters in the late 1700s in England. Unable to work, they must marry wealthy men to secure a comfortable future for themselves. The novel opens when a wealthy man moves to their village and their mother is desperate to meet him. This line iterates what all the characters want—a single, wealthy man, looking for a wife. |
| "All happy families are alike; every unhappy family is unhappy in its own way." (*Anna Karenina*) | This opening line introduces the idea of family drama by making a social observation. The stereotypical "happy family" is compared to the unique unhappiness that an individual can feel within their own family. Take a look at the precise sentence structure that makes it memorable: parallel sentences united by a semi-colon. |
| "Okonkwo was well known throughout the nine villages, and even beyond." (*Things Fall Apart*) | This opening line is successful in large part due to its frank tone and simplistic style. Okonkwo is the protagonist of *Things Fall Apart*, and the novel narrates both his personal downfall and the imperialization of the Igbo people by European colonizers. This sentence states Okonkwo's status, well known, and the setting of the novel, the nine villages. |

# ACTIVITY

Let's use these classic examples to draft a few options for your opening sentences.

1.  **Use a universally appealing statement to introduce your topic.**

_____

_____

_____

2.  **Use a semicolon to unite two sentences that compare and contrast a topic discussed in your essay.**

_____

_____

_____

3.  **Use frank, simple language to describe yourself and your community.**

_____

_____

_____

Let's take a look at what a Big Idea introduction looks like in practice. This essay is responding to the following prompt:

*Indicate a person who has had a significant influence on you, and describe that influence.*

A powerful opening sentence that immediately brings the reader into the essay.

Cynicism is a common byproduct of grieving, and my father's suicide forced me into its grip. Where did the eternal optimist who "always looked on the bright side" go? There is no bright side when you lose your best friend to tragedy. Fortunately, I have sixteen years of great memories with my father. This nostalgia has overcome my initial slide into bitterness and cynicism and it soothes me when I most miss my dad.

The author is revealing a core belief that is being challenged.

Rather than dwelling on death and cynicism, the final sentence shifts focus toward something more positive, which shows a forward-thinking mentality from the author.

Don't feel as if you need to write about a tragedy. Everyday experiences can be just as relatable and successful. What matters is that they're well written and insightful.

# ACTIVITY

## The More You Read, the Better You Write

The best writers tend also to be the best readers because they're always absorbing new ways in which to tell a story. To be clear, this doesn't mean that you should be imitating what others have done. Imitation might be the best form of flattery, but it does little to help you stand out. However, you *should* be taking notes on what works and considering how you might use those techniques to craft your own writing.

Here are a few examples from successful college essays. For each, underline the parts of each sentence that draw you in.

- "It is a statistical fact that about three percent of babies are born breech. It has not been determined, however, whether prenatal upside-downness affects spatial orientation during the rest of the baby's life. But in my case, reversed entry into the world appears responsible for at least one significant subsequent event."

- "Egyptian sarcophagi. Minoan vases. Ancient things speak to me. Their stories fascinate me. I feel a personal connection to people, places, and objects from before modern civilization; this is my passion."

- "Every day, the news is filled with stories of brilliant politicians and gorgeous Hollywood actors. Society chooses to give its million-dollar bills to football players and pop stars, and even my parents want me to jump on the bandwagon of fame and wealth by becoming a lawyer, a neurosurgeon, or a business magnate. Yet somehow, I know I would not feel quite right spending my life as a glamorous celebrity or an affluent doctor, but I hope to be a somebody someday. After all, who doesn't want to make their mom and dad proud?"

- "An awe-inspired fan once told a famous master of the flamenco style, "I would give my life to play as well as you do." The guitarist responded, "I already did." To me, music is the language of the mind, and the melodious arpeggio of a burnished walnut instrument speaks what cannot be written in words."

- "To really understand who I am, remember your childhood. Remember the pleasure that eating a great big peanut butter and jelly sandwich delivered? How it seemed to just slide down your throat and ease into your stomach? That sandwich is the result of the perfect combination of ingredients, all working together to create a satisfying experience. If any one ingredient was missing, the whole sandwich would fall apart. I would argue that the world is very much like one large PB&J, filled with many different ingredients."

# Start Mid-Splash

Another way to start the essay is to begin in the middle of a big splash, a technique known as *in medias res*. Though the Latin phrase, which means "in the middle of things," is old, this method is often used today, especially on television and in films. That's because the mind has a need to fill in the blanks, and if you leave a reader wondering how you got into the middle of a fight, they'll not only read on to see how it resolves, but to see how you wound up there in the first place.

The one caution is that *in medias res* openings tend to take up an entire paragraph—they're hard to compress into a sentence or two. As a result, you may need to find a clever way to introduce the topic and characterize yourself while you're also describing the dramatic effect of the scene.

"I love to see essays that grab my attention right from the beginning. A student's ability to use descriptors and dialogue is quite effective. Additionally, it's great when students stick to the topic and keep the essay concise."

—Quinnipiac University

To build your own *in medias res* opening, follow these steps:

## ❶ Start with the climax.

What is the most exciting moment of the experience(s) you're recounting in your essay? Use a climactic moment, a conflict, or a sudden revelation as your starting point. Then describe it in as much visceral detail as possible to make it real for the reader.

## ❷ Play catch up.

As your essay progresses, give context so your reader understands the situation you began with. Focus on your personal experiences, interests, and/or choices that led to the starting point. Use clear transitional phrases, such as "Before this…" or "Two months prior…".

## ❸ Reflect. Reflect. Reflect.

It's easy to get caught up in plot and drama, particularly if you have a knack for fiction writing. Keep bringing things back to the prompt, using the action to emphasize who you are as a unique college applicant.

Here's a sample of a Mid-Splash opening. See if you can figure out what the prompt was!

**Three different types of action quickly establish the climactic, chaotic scene.**

**Each new detail plays catch up, allowing the reader to fill in the gaps. The author could've simply described a concert, but now we feel as if we're a part of it.**

**Though it's written in the present tense, this still serves as a reflection, introducing the writer's emotional connection to music.**

**Pay attention to both uses of time; they enhance one another.**

**Notice how the author holds their involvement back to add to the mystery of the story.**

**Not just any music, but a tune from *Star Wars*, a cultural touchstone to help orient readers and inform them about the writer's tastes.**

His arms flew through the hot summer air. There was a deafening delay. Someone shouted, "We love you!" Was it me? Snapping open my camera, I focused intently on his expression. Suddenly, the blistering B-flat chord thundered from the platform and applause spread through the crowd like an electrical current. The musical rush of *Star Wars* was contagious. For two minutes and fifty-five seconds, the Blossom Musical Festival audience was mesmerized, and I realized why I had convinced my family to drive eight hours for the moment. His music, in its grandeur and consonance, was perfect. *I want to tell him how it makes me feel!*

# ACTIVITY

## What's Going On?

For each of the following sample *in medias res* introductions, see how quickly you can correctly identify what's actually happening. Underline each new clue and circle the one that gives it away to you.

- "Many times when I thought that I could not go any further, I had to rely on all of my inner strength to pull myself through. This summer I spent eight weeks on a bicycle that carried not only me, but all of my worldly possessions for those eight weeks, from Seattle, Washington, to Sea Bright, New Jersey. I moved my legs around in constant circles for seven or eight hours a day, every day, all the way from the Pacific to the Atlantic."

- "Beat her up," one of them shrieked, referring to me, while the four of them pounded their fists into their hands on the sidewalk corner. I had suggested that we run faster, but my cross-country teammates' response demonstrated that they didn't agree. Although they were entirely kidding about the violence, such a strong statement was quite frustrating."

- "I looked into the microscope and gracefully fumbled around with the tweezers and scissors, attempting to assist my lab mentor tie two arteries together."

- "Click. Click. The last two feet fall into position with 42 others, thus ending the procession of shoes and leaving only their echo to fill the ancient stone monastery. Slowly, even this remnant of sound departs the room and only an expectant silence is left. For a brief moment, there is no motion, no breath, no sound. Then, almost imperceptibly, twenty-two pairs of eyes rotate upwards, each following the arc of one hand in its purposeful rise. Suddenly an organ chord bursts through the silence. The single hand sweeps downwards, three rows of mouths open, and the concert begins."

# END OF CHAPTER REVIEW

Solving math equations and identifying historical facts are problems that have right or wrong answers. There's no one way to write, however, which can be a bit scary. How do you know when your essay is ready?

Ultimately, you know when you know. Read each draft as critically as you can, and keep assessing whether you've shown enough or if there's still room for growth.

Below, shade in how complete you feel each section of your personal statement is. Beneath each progress bar, even the ones you may have filled out at 100%, write at least *one* thing you can try adding, whether it's a new detail or a different stylistic approach.

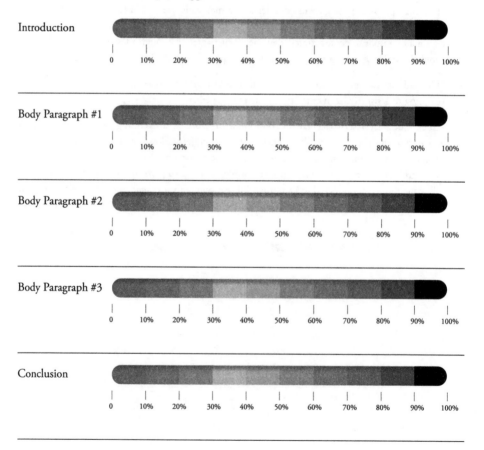

Introduction

| 0 | 10% | 20% | 30% | 40% | 50% | 60% | 70% | 80% | 90% | 100% |

Body Paragraph #1

| 0 | 10% | 20% | 30% | 40% | 50% | 60% | 70% | 80% | 90% | 100% |

Body Paragraph #2

| 0 | 10% | 20% | 30% | 40% | 50% | 60% | 70% | 80% | 90% | 100% |

Body Paragraph #3

| 0 | 10% | 20% | 30% | 40% | 50% | 60% | 70% | 80% | 90% | 100% |

Conclusion

| 0 | 10% | 20% | 30% | 40% | 50% | 60% | 70% | 80% | 90% | 100% |

# Chapter 4: Choosing Your Tone

## How to Find the Right Voice for a College Admissions Officer

Think about some of your favorite songs and the parts of them that stand out. In the last chapter, we looked at some techniques for how you might use hooks to catch the audience's attention. Here, we'll look at how you can modulate your written "voice" to keep the reader engaged. This is true of movie directors, pop stars, even fashion designers. Finding that unique angle—that personal flair—is what distinguishes the ordinary from the extraordinary.

Even if you don't think of yourself as an artist, you can still apply artistic techniques to your personal statement and writing in general. In this chapter, you'll learn how to:

- choose between formal and informal writing

- find, amplify, and modify your voice

- pick the perfect details

- properly apply humor

# SPEAK FROM THE HEART

Some people are born with a natural ability to tear their hearts off their sleeves and slap them down on the page. The real trick is for the rest of us to be as open with our essays. Have no fear. Here are few great ways to get started.

- **Write a letter** to someone you haven't spoken to in a while. Do it by hand, using a pen and notebook. Sit on the floor, writing on your knees. It should feel almost like writing a diary.

- **Play with index cards**. Try writing a sentence on an index card. Then write the same sentence on another index card, using a different style. Think of this a bit like the glass of water being half empty or half full; if you've described something using a negative tone, try rewriting it from a more positive outlook. Do this a few times to play around with how the same ideas seem to change along with the mood.

- **Speak your first draft**. This works well for some people instead of writing. In fact, there are fiction writers who have composed many books without ever writing a word. To find out if this is your strength, speak your thoughts to somebody, and if you get a good response, then write down the same words that you just spoke. It's that simple. If you don't like to write or type, ask someone—a friend, a sibling, someone you're blackmailing—to take transcription for you. (We're kidding about that blackmail part.) If it's available, you might also consider using professional voice-to-text transcription software.

- **Storyboard your personal statement.** Storyboarding is a technique used for many films, particularly animated ones, where you illustrate the major moments of your story so that you can see how to get from one point to the next. This can be especially helpful for visual storytellers, but is also useful if you find yourself losing focus.

Try one, two, three, or even all four of these. See what works best!

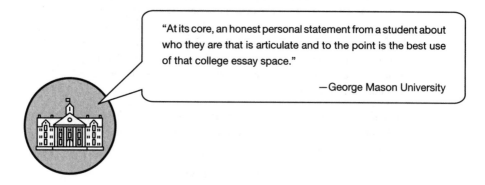

"At its core, an honest personal statement from a student about who they are that is articulate and to the point is the best use of that college essay space."

—George Mason University

# ACTIVITY

### No, Seriously, *Speak* from Your Heart

Choose a voice-to-text transcription software (like Google Keyboard, which is free), or just record yourself with a microphone or your phone. Now, speak for at least two minutes on the following prompt, without holding anything back:

*What is the most memorable meal I've ever eaten?*

Once you're done, listen to your recording or read the transcript. Take the three sentences that felt most honest to you and write them below.

_____

_____

_____

_____

_____

Now choose one of the sentences above to write as a warning, one to write as a funny story, and one to write as an important secret, and fill those in below. (You may notice that some sentences are easier to adapt than others.)

As a warning to someone:

_____

_____

As a funny story:

_____

_____

As an important secret:

_____

_____

# THE DIFFERENCE BETWEEN FORMAL AND INFORMAL TONE

Normally, academic essays are written in a formal, professional style. But your college essay is an exception to the rule, because above all, the reader wants to get to know *you*, which means that your writing should be personal, even if that means being a little informal.

The trick is to avoid crossing any inappropriate lines, or to go too far in any one direction. And the best way to do that—to be informal without forgetting that it's formal—is to fully understand how each type of tone works.

## Formal Tone

Listing all the elements that constitute a formal tone would fill this entire book. Let's limit it to the most relevant stuff. For college application essays, a formal tone should include the following:

- varied types of sentences, veering toward longer (instead of shorter)

- varied types of diction, veering toward sophisticated (instead of simple)

- active voice

- use of *such as* (instead of *like*)

- use of *completely* (instead of *totally*)]

Read the following paragraph and see if you can identify any of the above elements:

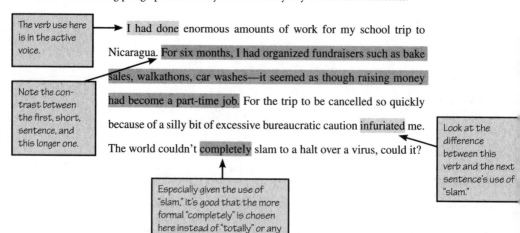

The verb use here is in the active voice.

I had done enormous amounts of work for my school trip to Nicaragua. For six months, I had organized fundraisers such as bake sales, walkathons, car washes—it seemed as though raising money had become a part-time job. For the trip to be cancelled so quickly because of a silly bit of excessive bureaucratic caution infuriated me. The world couldn't completely slam to a halt over a virus, could it?

Note the contrast between the first, short, sentence, and this longer one.

Look at the difference between this verb and the next sentence's use of "slam."

Especially given the use of "slam," it's good that the more formal "completely" is chosen here instead of "totally" or any other informal adverb.

# Informal Tone

Unless you were raised by nineteenth-century Brit lit professors, you know what an informal tone is. Most of us speak informally every day of our lives.

The problem is that there are limits to that informality on your personal statement and especially on supplemental essays. Here are some tips.

**Avoid curse words.** This should be obvious. Even if swearing is central to your story or anecdote, you don't have to be strictly verbatim. Consider how much more interesting it is to read "From my brother's mouth came a silky string of obscenities that nobody could quite believe" as opposed to the obscenity itself.

**Avoid sarcasm.** On the page or screen, sarcasm looks exactly the same as sincerity! Sarcasm itself is transmitted through non-written stuff like voice, mannerisms, and shared history, so keep it out of college applications where it may be misunderstood.

**Avoid using real names.** Talking about an unusual friend or acquaintance is totally fine, but don't use his or her real name. Assign a fake name! After all, your friend might be applying to the same university, and that could cause massive awkwardness.

**Avoid vague or basic verbs.** Experienced admission officials often look at your verbs to see what kind of thinker you are. Sticking to a basic set of verbs like *got* or *is* limits both your vocabulary and what readers are able to learn about you.

 Your essay is, above all else, an *opportunity* for you to show how you stand out. A common curse or petulant tone isn't anything new, but the creative way in which you write around such vague, basic, or overused expressions can be!

It may be easier to see the difference between verb choices by looking at some examples. Each of the following sentences has been rewritten to eliminate the vague or basic verbs and replace them with more descriptive ones.

*Vague or basic:* After that, I <u>got</u> an A on my final paper, and it <u>felt</u> so good.

*Specific:* After that, I <u>earned</u> an A on my final paper, an experience that <u>counts</u> as one of the crowning moments of my junior year.

*Vague or basic:* My father <u>is</u> one of the strongest people I know, and he <u>is</u> one of the better mechanics out there too.

*Specific:* My father, one of the strongest people I know, <u>has built</u> a reputation as an even better mechanic.

Here's a longer form example of how shifts to individual sentences can carry over throughout an entire essay. Read both essays, then carefully look at the differences, and not just the ones we've already called out!

## Formal

The mother is not the subject—her problems are. This passively removes blame from the mother.

Contrast this formal usage with the informal one on the next page.

Navigating my mother's moods occupied years of my life. While she tried her best to raise me, her problems often resulted in the reverse: I often was forced to guide our lives. Then, our relationship took a more serious turn two years ago, when she attended a 90-day rehabilitation program for alcoholism.

Formal verb usages such as "descend the staircase," if desired, can be written more informally.

I would be lying if I said that this event had surprised me. On many school nights, after I finished my homework, I would descend the staircase, shut off the television, throw away the empty liquor bottle, and lift my drunken parent onto my shoulder. As I hoisted her upstairs to bed, she would awaken and insist on carrying herself the rest of the way.

Passive verb construction is a formal choice. Contrast this with how the next essay handles this construction.

A direct quotation is quite formal.

Nothing was ever said, no apologies were ever uttered. This was simply the way things were during my ninth and tenth grade years. I had no power over the situation, and so I lived according to that famous prayer. I asked God to "grant me the serenity to accept the things I cannot change."

My mother came back from the rehabilitation facility a very different woman. The nights of drinking were gone, replaced by a deep obsession with following recommended videos on YouTube. Her already short temper became nonexistent, and she moved around the house in a constant state of agitation. I had traded one problematic mother for a different problematic mother.

# Informal

I was young—knee-high to a coffee table, as my uncle would say—when I realized that my mother had problems. I can tell you that she tried her best to raise me, but the honest truth is that she failed. I ended up being the parent in our relationship. That is, until our relationship took a nosedive two years ago, after she checked into a 90-day rehabilitation program for people addicted to adult juice. That's what she called alcohol.

> Unlike "her problems often resulted," this is the direct active voice, and it puts blame squarely on the mother's shoulders.

> This is much more informal than "took a more serious turn."

> Cute nicknames are another sign of informality.

It wasn't any surprise—no way, absolutely not. Most of the time, after I finished my homework, I would go downstairs, shut off the television, throw away the empty liquor bottle, and lift my passed-out mother onto my shoulder. She would wake up before we reached the bedroom and try to twist away. She didn't like me to carry her all the way to bed.

> An em dash followed by a childish "no way"? This is informal to the max!

She never said sorry. Not for any of it. This was simply the way things were during my ninth and tenth grade. I couldn't do a single stupid thing about us, so I just said that famous prayer to myself, the one where you ask God to give you the serenity to accept the things you can't change.

> Fragments are permitted!

> An indirect quotation—reported speech—can be more informal, and even preferable.

My mom came back from the rehabilitation facility, and—wow—was she different. No more booze—her new obsession was YouTube, and she fell down those rabbit holes until the sun came up on the horizon. Her temper grew awful. She'd snap at me for the massive sin of leaving a dirty butter knife on the counter. She stumbled around the house muttering to herself. It was an even trade, as far as I was concerned—one bad mom for another. At least the new one didn't smell like stale booze.

> Conversational interjections? Hey! That's informal!

> Metaphorical language is usually informal.

> Be careful deploying sarcasm like this. It's not usually advisable.

> Beware getting too personal when using an informal voice. The language here reads angry and bitter, which might raise flags to the reader.

# When to Use Informal Language

Right now, you might feel totally jittery about crossing linguistic lines that you probably weren't even thinking about. Relax! Just as there are certain topics to avoid, there are also certain words and phrasings to steer clear of. On the whole, however, informal language is not only allowed, it is encouraged.

## First-person Pronouns

Did you grow up feeling that if you ever turned in a paper with an "I" that you would be booted out of school? You're not alone. Here's the truth: Yes, you can use first-person pronouns such as "I" in your personal statement. Teachers tend to crack down hard on that kind of usage because it can lead students to make unsupported statements rather than to rely on the facts at hand. But in this case, the facts at hand are about you: remember, it's a *personal* statement.

*Formal:* The student sat at the desk, thinking long and hard about what to write.

*Informal:* I sat there, swiveling in my chair, trying to come up with the right words.

You don't have to use something just because you can. Try to avoid the same repetitious constructions, as they suggest a laziness to your writing or, worse, will make you seem self-absorbed.

## Contractions

As with the first-person, teachers tend to shun contractions because they can lead to your papers sounding conversational, as opposed to carefully researched or diligently argued. But your college applications is, to some degree, a conversation between you and the reader. If a contraction helps you set a mood or better communicate a topic, it's—see what we did there?—up to you.

*Formal:* It is very difficult to write well when you are tired, so do not stay up all night.

*Informal:* It's very difficult to write well when you're tired, so don't pull an all-nighter.

The reason many of these usages are okay is because they're still grammatically correct; they're just informal. You can use "it's" or "it is," but don't accidentally use the possessive "its" when you mean "it is" or, worse, "its'"—a word that doesn't exist.

## Reported Dialogue

Teachers usually drill the use of quotes for dialogue because they want to make sure that their students understand how to properly cite a source. They cared at least as much about the accuracy of the statements as the underlying story. But because the personal statement is from your point of view and often from your memory, you're free to report what someone said instead of quoting it.

> *Formal:* "PewDiePie made the best vlogs," said my sister. "Then he lost his mind."

> *Informal:* My sister believes that PewDiePie made the best vlogs until he lost his mind.

Don't dismiss quotes entirely! They can help to make a conversation easier to follow and, if properly used, help to distinguish your essay. Just critically think about whether each element of your essay is useful, and avoid too much of any one style.

## Fragments

As long as they are used artfully, by which we mean with intent, fragments are okay. You can't just. Add random punctuation. You should, however, feel free to use them the same way that fiction writers do: to change the rhythm of the sentence or to shake up the structure of a list.

> *Formal:* Reasons to avoid a trip to Nepal include the weather, the risk of avalanches, and the overpriced guides.

> *Informal:* There were many reasons to avoid a trip to Nepal. Weather. Avalanches. Guides. Guides! There were some good ones, but I'd only ever found them to be overpriced.

Rhythm can be particularly important in an essay. Remember that these readers are going through multiple essays in a row. An effective shift in tone that forces readers to slow down or focus on something can help them remember *your* essay.

## Miscellaneous

There are plenty of other rules you've been taught that would still be grammatically correct if broken. Like starting a sentence with a conjunction or preposition! Or ending with one, like so. Believe it or not, your teachers have been drilling these rules into your head so that you know when and how to *break* them.

> *Formal:* Samantha made a turkey-swiss-and-avocado sandwich because she felt hungry.

> *Informal:* Because Samantha felt hungry, she made a turkey-swiss-and-avocado sandwich.

Before you look at the annotations to the paragraph below, see if you can figure out what's being done and whether you find it effective or not.

<table>
<tr><td>First-person pronoun and contraction. Two for one! Both usually indicate informality, especially the contraction.</td><td>I'd been worried about my second-semester physics project ever since that meeting with my counselor. In between bites of baby carrots and hummus, she'd told me that the last person to attempt something this ambitious was a girl everybody called The Caffeineator. I remembered her and she was an extreme character. Hyperactive. Controlling. Brilliant.</td><td>Reported dialogue. This is often more informal than reporting the dialogue directly.</td></tr>
</table>

First-person pronoun and contraction. Two for one! Both usually indicate informality, especially the contraction.

I'd been worried about my second-semester physics project ever since that meeting with my counselor. In between bites of baby carrots and hummus, she'd told me that the last person to attempt something this ambitious was a girl everybody called The Caffeineator. I remembered her and she was an extreme character. Hyperactive. Controlling. Brilliant.

Reported dialogue. This is often more informal than reporting the dialogue directly.

Three fragments, three bits of informality.

# ACTIVITY

## A Tone for All Seasons

Rewrite the following informal paragraphs to create a **formal** tone. Remove curse words, sarcasm, real names, and simple or vague verbs. Add active voice, vary the syntax (focusing on longer sentences), and add one or two more sophisticated vocabulary words.

a)  It felt like it took forever but my Uncle Joe finally said, "Look, you're too smart to be hanging around with those boys down at the dump." *Whatever,* I thought. I was so cocky then. Arrogant.

_____

_____

b)  *Who's the GOAT?* I told myself. I said it over and over and over again. It's so important to always be telling yourself those kinds of things. It's not even fair how some people are just born with that self-confidence. Not me, I have to earn it.

_____

_____

_____

Rewrite the following paragraphs to create a more **informal** tone. Add contractions, first-person pronouns, attributed dialogue, and fragments.

a) My team's soccer coach, Hal Merrington, was screaming from the sidelines: "Play the ball to Bryan! No railroad tracks! Give and go!" He originally hailed from England, and few were those who could easily understand him. There were many rumors about Coach Hal, some of which were accurate and others that were less accurate. Some said that he had been a taxi driver, while others said that he had been a roadie for the Rolling Stones. A credible rumor was that Coach Hal had played with West Ham United, in the Premier League, for a few months before being cut.

_____

_____

_____

_____

_____

_____

_____

b) Vaulting itself from zilch to a revered citywide event in a mind-boggling twelve months, the Value Volleyball tournament could be viewed as my brainchild; more specifically, it has been portrayed by those closest to me as a channel through which my deepest yearnings as a person of athletic strength could express his myriad needs for community participation and public excellence.

_____

_____

_____

_____

_____

For these last two paragraphs, first *identify* whether it's **formal** or **informal** <u>and then rewrite each in the opposite style.</u>

a)    In my head, the offending passage could've been anything, an arpeggio, a prechorus, a single discordant note. But it wasn't clear what sounded so horrible or why.

_____

_____

b)    Before I knew it, my friend Renee fell flat on her face. "Nice job," I said. "You're such a jerk," she replied. We had a weird relationship. It wasn't like the others, it was open flirty, more so than with others, but we both knew that it wouldn't ever be more than that. Kissing her would've been as gross as kissing my sister!

_____

_____

_____

## FINDING YOUR VOICE

Have you ever heard a brand-new song—and without looking at your playlist, from just the opening chords, or perhaps from the first word, you knew exactly who made it?

Some people have a very identifiable voice. If you're one of those unicorns, then congratulations. So long as you choose the right topic and don't break the wrong rules, your personal statement will likely stand out, though it's still on you to make sure the college admissions officers *like* what they're reading.

Most of us, however, don't have a strong written voice. That's not a problem if you're writing technical manuals or scientific research; those are places where a lack of personal voice is necessary. For example:

*The corrected instructions regarding the process of decontaminating the intake valve prior to desalinization can be found in section 7.8 of the Fourth Edition of the official Field Manual.*

But a personal statement is different. It needs your personality. It needs to show the admissions committee your quirks, oddities, and weird observations. These are not to be hidden or ironed out—display them!

For your first drafts, go overboard with your voice. It is much easier to edit a statement to make it more conservative than it is to try and find your voice on the second pass!

Here is one anecdote:

> When I was in Madrid one time, an American girl walked into the restaurant. She said in Spanish that she wanted a churro and hot chocolate, but the man behind the counter didn't understand her because of her accent. I translated for her, and he brought her the churro and chocolate. She didn't say anything. It taught me that practicing languages can really help people.

Does it leave you flat? Here is another version of the same anecdote:

> "Yo quiero un chocolate con churro," the American girl said, "por favor."
>
> She was dressed in ratty red sweatpants and her hair hung in a sloppy ponytail. A wad of gum snapped in her mouth. She looked like my seventh-grade sister when she's lying on the couch on a miserable Saturday afternoon in February, eyes glued to her phone. But we were in a fashionable Madrid bar, and I felt sorry for this stranger because the man behind the counter clearly had zero idea what she was saying. So I repeated her order the best I could, using my newfound fluid Madrileño accent. He understood and quickly brought her the hot chocolate and churro. She looked upset and went to the other side of the room without thanking me. I didn't care. I was too hungry to care about anything except getting that plate of fried shrimp goodness.

Sensory description for the win!

Comparisons are a very effective way to describe things with a personal touch, but make sure they're understandable. Had this author just said "like my seventh-grade sister," the reader would be missing context. The remainder gives us that vital context about her casualness and her phone fixation.

Reconstructed dialogue is very professional. A little goes a long way, though.

Don't forget to track the emotional state of your main character, which is you. This is easy to forget for applicants who are overly brainy. Emotions matter!

What does the second version have that the first one lacked?

- a lot of sensory description

- references to the writer's emotional state

- a comparison

- a direct quotation (which is okay, if it brings specificity)

- no moral of the story (lets the story speak for itself)

A personal statement that doesn't reveal your personality is forgettable—and that is the biggest problem of all!

# ACTIVITY

Rewrite both of the following anecdotes in a way that highlights your personal voice. Don't focus on each individual sentence—your voice might not emphasize all of the points in these samples. Do, however, try to stick to the same subject, much as you will have to stick to your chosen topic.

> It was disappointing when my principal read the name of the winner of the contest out loud. It had been a lot of hard work but ultimately I had not won the prize. I was very sad and that night I didn't really feel like doing my homework, or anything else. So my mom took me to my favorite restaurant to cheer me up. It worked. I was back to normal the next day. My mother is very loving, and she always knows how to build me up—she's always going to be my biggest fan.

My interest in physics has been very long and intense. I have been studying the topic ever since I was little, and my family members have always encouraged me. They don't really know much about physics because I am the first person in my family to apply to college, but my father says that he used to dream about me becoming a famous physicist while he was working in the kitchen of his restaurant. I don't want to disappoint him, so I have always worked very hard to be the best that I can be.

_____

_____

_____

_____

_____

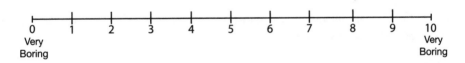

# THE DETAILS

Selection of details is key. This isn't a scale from 0 to 10 where 0 means that a lack of details has led to a boring essay, but 10 means that a surplus of details has created a captivating one. The scale actually looks like this:

```
├──┼──┼──┼──┼──┼──┼──┼──┼──┼──┤
0   1  2  3  4  5  6  7  8  9  10
Very                          Very
Boring                      Boring
```

Both extremes result in a negative outcome, which means the sweet spot is in the middle. Professional writers learn, over months and years of practice, exactly where that sweet spot lives. They discover which details to leave in and which to leave out. For now, as with your voice, fill your early drafts with as many details as you can think of. Just be prepared to cut many of them as you edit.

If you've taken creative writing classes, you've probably heard the expression "Kill your darlings." No, creative writers aren't secretly a bunch of bloodthirsty murders! They are, however, expected to recognize when their favorite lines just aren't working and need to be cut.

# Brain Types

Some types of brains see in less sensory detail than others. Future engineers, for example, often write with no detail because they're so focused on abstract process. These personal statements tend to be dry as a result.

Other types of brains see too much sensory detail. Many artists, for example, are open to the world. When they decide to fill the page with detail, it can be overwhelming. And then there are completist brains, which catalogue and record as much as possible.

Your job is to find a balance between all of these.

When describing a new person, place, or thing, make a separate list of adjectives or details that describe it or them, and then try to narrow it down to the most relevant single detail. Add only if a reader wouldn't understand, and only then if you can't think of a more precise word that might help you sum the noun up.

Here's what it looks like when there aren't enough details:

> When we finally arrived at the debate tournament, we were totally exhausted. We looked terrible. We all forgot to set the alarm, so Mr. Linder had to wake us up the next morning and we barely made it to the tournament. (41 words)

Notice the lack of sensory information and concrete nouns. It has no specificity. Your eyes glide past the paragraph without lingering over anything.

Now let's flip the script. Here is the same story with way, way, way too many details:

Our flight to the debate tournament arrived four hours late because a passenger in row 27 decided they needed to get something from their stowed baggage RIGHT THEN, and refused to sit down. So we had to make an emergency landing in Kansas City, kick out the unruly passenger, and then wait while the staff filed a report on the man's behavior. Finally we took off and continued onwards to Austin. By the time we had pulled up to the gate, disembarked (which took forever), got our bags at the baggage claim, found our van, and driven to the center of the city, it was already three o'clock in the morning. Check-in was slow that time of night, so it was 4:15 before our heads hit the pillows. I had to share a saggy queen bed with Ryan, one above and one below the sheets. It was weird enough sleeping in the same bed as a friend, especially one who snores louder than a piece of farm equipment. It's hard to believe that people shared beds with strangers all the time in the nineteenth century—that's actually where we get the term "strange bedfellows." Anyways, I had trouble falling asleep so I stared at the ceiling for at least an hour, imagining that the little swirls in the panels were like chocolate chip cookie dough ice cream, which is my favorite, though I think many could say the same. By the time we fell asleep, nobody had remembered to set an alarm—well, actually, Timmy did set his, but he accidentally set it for 7:00 pm. Coach Linder pounded on the door at 8:00 the next morning and shocked us out of bed. We didn't have any time to shower or brush our teeth or drink water. We just leapt out of bed, put on our suits, and did our ties in the elevator downstairs. When the elevator doors opened at the mezzanine level, we bolted out and ran to the ballroom to find our room assignments. (353 words)

The key difference between the two, from a drafting perspective, is that you can at least get a sense of the story being told in the second example. There are too many extraneous details in the second version—the use of the word "Anyways" is a clear sign that someone has gotten off-topic—but at least you can focus now on cutting.

Ask yourself "What's the story that I want to tell?" and then circle the supporting details. Keep what works and revise as necessary. If it's still too long, answer the question more specifically to further pare things down. Here's an example of how this story might read as a finished body paragraph:

> Our flight had unfortunately been delayed by an unruly passenger who had to be deposited in Kansas City. By the time we burst into our hotel room in Austin, it was already 4:15 in the morning. A loud pounding on the door the next morning jerked me awake. It was Coach Linder, screaming. Timmy had accidentally set our alarm for 7:00 pm, and we'd overslept by an hour. Unshowered, filthy from the night before, we leapt out of bed, threw on our suits, and raced downstairs to the ballroom to find our room assignments. The debate tournament was about to begin. (102 words)

To borrow from a children's story—this porridge is not too hot, not too cold. It's just right.

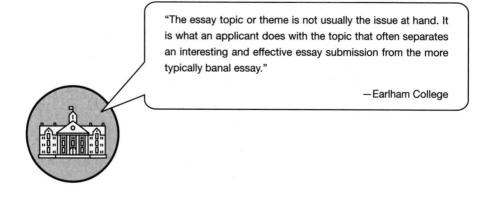

"The essay topic or theme is not usually the issue at hand. It is what an applicant does with the topic that often separates an interesting and effective essay submission from the more typically banal essay."

—Earlham College

Read the following essay excerpt and think about what works and doesn't work for you, then go back and read the annotations. Don't feel as if you *have* to make changes like this in your own work, but at least be aware of the decisions you are making not to, so that your essay reads with purpose and voice.

This is a vague beginning. Who s the other co-chair? What organization? Consider instead the more active "As the co-chair of our school's chapter of Habitat for Humanity, I had spent..."

When introducing topics, always consider how much information is necessary. The focus here stays on the work the student is doing as opposed to getting bogged down in descriptions of a national nonprofit.

The other co-chair and I had spent all winter planning the trip to Louisiana with our school's chapter of Habitat For Humanity. We were going to help rebuild homes after Hurricane Katrina. True, that disaster had devastated the region ten years earlier, but the regional director of the organization told me that they were still rebuilding.

We had seven students signed up, so we rented a big passenger van. One of the parents volunteered to chaperone and found four rooms in a cheap motel. We bought a large box of instant noodles to save money. As the time drew closer, I grew less confident in my decision. Were we really going paint walls and hammer shingles on a roof in the swampy humidity?

I wanted to back out. But the person who reminded me of my responsibility, of finishing what you start, was my aunt.

What's the important detail? If it's trying to keep down the costs, the number of rooms is worth mentioning. If it's about the people in the rooms, it might be better to state that there were two people to a room.

Here, the impact of the hurricane is being described as it pertains to the work the writer would be doing for the organization. Always aim for personal context!

This isn't just a detail of the type of work—it also emphasizes the narrator's indecision because it's phrased as a question. Always keep an eye out for places like this where you can do more.

# ACTIVITY

## Getting It *Just* Right

Rewrite the following paragraphs with an appropriate amount of detail. Though these likely aren't your experiences, try to identify which details *would* be important to you, and condense or expand them. In other words, keep the structure while adding or subtracting details.

**Too Long**

Standing there in the classroom, with blue, red, and green dry erase markers in my hand, I looked down at the little boy, who was not even four years old. His name was Erik, but everybody called him Captain Crybaby, including the teacher, Mrs. Schmittel, privately. I heard that Erik's mother had been an opera singer who now was battling multiple sclerosis. I don't know anything about his father, if he was even present. Erik was staring at me with two crayons shoved up his nostrils, his little lower lip jutting outwards like a boxer daring a fight. He'd tied a cape around his shoulders. His long-sleeved shirt was soaked up to the elbows with snot. I noticed that his Velcro shoes were old and barely hanging onto his feet. He stood there, a tiny king daring me to defy him. Then, as I watched, he snatched a pair of blunt red plastic scissors from a little girl and charged at me. I caught his hand and diverted the sharp instrument away just before it drove into my crotch. He started crying and stamping his feet and screaming. I saw snot bubbling from his nose and saliva from his mouth. I didn't know if I should touch him or not because he seemed like a tiny contaminated germ factory. This was my first week as a teacher's aide, here in room 204, and I was sure it was going to be my last.

**Just Right**

_____

_____

_____

_____

_____

_____

**Too Short**

My grandfather told me to come over on Friday because he had a surprise for me. He never gave surprises to me or my sisters. I wondered what it could be, and it was hard to sleep that week because I kept wondering. That Friday I got to his house and he was sitting outside on the porch. He pointed at his old car in the street and said, "That's yours."

**Just Right**

_____

_____

_____

_____

_____

_____

# HUMOR

Evaluate this joke:

*A man walked into a bar ... and said ouch.*

Funny? Not funny? It depends on context. To people who've heard a lot of *A man walked into a bar* jokes, this rates pretty high on the funny meter. To people who've never heard this type of joke, it's mildly funny. To other people, it's just plain dumb.

We hate to repeat a point, as we mentioned this back in Chapter 1, but humor is largely dependent on context. That context includes many things, such as geography, language, age, and even time—the moment at which a joke is delivered will change its reception. What makes humor so high stakes, particularly in a personal statement, is that the cost of offending a reader with a joke that's in poor taste far outweighs any gain from amusing another reader. Think long and hard about the possible effect your joke may have and remember that you won't be in the room to explain yourself, so make sure it can't be misinterpreted.

The target of the joke also matters. It's one thing to be self-deprecating and to find humor in your *own* situation, but it's another to mean-spiritedly mock someone else. That shows a lack of character.

## So, What's Up, Princeton Review?

So yes, you *can* use humor in your personal statement. The question is whether you *should*. To answer that, you need to honestly decide if humor is a natural part of your voice. If you're already doing stand-up routines, writing jokes for your school's newspaper, or would be described as the class clown or life of the party, you might want to give it a try.

If the people in your life *do* find you funny, you'll want to determine *what* makes them laugh. Is it physical comedy? Is it lowbrow humor? Unless the point of your essay is to show how your humor evolved or landed you a notable opportunity on a respected website, you might want to hold back on certain types of jokes. Your readers are likely going to be older and wiser than your peers, so even if your friends laugh at your jokes, this might not be the best time or place to make someone you've never met crack up.

Humor doesn't always mean big laughs. One pun, a funny analogy, or even a sassy rejoinder can produce a moment of lightheartedness, which can be a relief to the reader if you're handling an otherwise weighty topic.

## So, Where's Up, Princeton Review?

Once you've decided to include humor, know that it doesn't matter *where* you put it. If you find yourself second-guessing whether a joke is appropriate in the first sentence, second paragraph, or conclusion, what you're really questioning is whether that joke is appropriate at all, in which case the answer is no, it's not.

The *amount* of humor, however, does matter. Remember, you want your personal statement to honestly reveal something about yourself. By being overly lighthearted, you can make it difficult for the reader to connect to you. Humor is, like everything else we've talked about in this chapter, a device to help you stand out. Overusing it, just like being too informal or too detail-oriented, can wear down a reader.

When you should use humor to show the reader something not in your transcript. If you suspect that you come off as an arrogant know-it-all, add a moment of self-deprecating humor. If you have a reputation as a slacker who can't settle on any one thing, then try a joke about how Shakespeare never signed his name the same way twice. (That's true, by the way, and is not actually a joke.)

If you do choose to employ humor, test it out on a counselor or teacher—someone likely to be a peer of the average college admissions reader. Watch their reaction as they read it; you should see a smile, some kind of delight.

The author is trying to make a humorous contrast, but be careful to what extremes you go, especially as many athletes have wound up in this situation. A better attempt might be to pull from something unrelated and unexpected: "I could've stepped into an alternate dimension where every food tasted like cinnamon."

Be careful not to set the bar too high—no pun intended! Unless what follows is actually depicted in an epic way, saying that it will be is setting yourself up for failure.

The first time I ever tried the high jump was a disaster of epic proportions.

It could've gone worse. After all, I could've ended up paralyzed! The first step in my flight to ignominy occurred at 4:00 pm on a Saturday—the occasion of my first track meet. I was wearing high-cut shorts that displayed my pasty, chunky white thighs to the world. I took a deep breath, then began my trip into hell.

Avoid being cruel, including to yourself.

If you have to keep telling (or explaining) the joke, it isn't a good one. We know it was a "disaster of epic proportions." We know it "could've gone worse." By this point, we want to know exactly what was so bad.

First, I did the bunny hop that my coach had showed me, where you do a bizarre vertical movement that kind of looks like an exaggeration of a person running in slow-motion. Then came the acceleration, which was barely perceptible in my case. Then came the planting of the foot—and the launch—

Be careful not to use too much self-deprecation. The readers want to see that you have some pride and some confidence.

Oh, but there was a problem. It'd just rained, and the asphalt was slick. I planted my foot, but it unfortunately had other ideas.

Personifying the foot is a good use of self-deprecation. There's already been a bit too much in this essay of that, but at least this is taking a different tack, and in a way that actually paints a funny picture.

That's certainly a vivid example! Consider whether the negatively charged word "rancid" helps or hurts.

The cursed little thing slid out from underneath me, and I went down to the ground like a sack of rancid butter. My body, now horizontal, collided with the thick mat. To make matters worse, the bar itself fell off its holder and hit me in the head. *Looney Tunes* couldn't have scripted it better.

When making references, be sure to use ones that the majority of readers would be able to get. Looney Tunes, which has been around for decades, is something accessible to all audiences.

# ACTIVITY

In each of the following paragraphs, underline the things that are funny, and then identify whether the overall tone and topic are appropriate or not.

> Looking at the red D at the top of my essay, I felt filled with indescribable rage. Mrs. Mooney was a bona fide witch. She was about ninety-nine years old and walked around in front of our class in her unbearable stupid sunflower sweater with her nose tilted up in the air. Clearly she believed that she pooped lavender brownies. But the fact was that she was a bitter, angry, miserable old woman who liked to penalize intelligent students just because she liked to be sadistic.

Appropriate or inappropriate?

_____

_____

> One thing that most people don't know about me is that I am a terrible cook. It's embarrassing. My family refuses to eat anything I make. A tray of cookies inevitably slides out looking like a volcanic landscape of burned rocks. Without supervision, I could burn water. I break into a cold sweat just looking at a spatula. It's a truly serious problem, and it makes me feel utterly inadequate. I'm not sure if I'm emphasizing this enough. When I get older and live on my own, I don't know what I'm going to do. I'll probably just buy hot dogs from street vendors and sodas from 7–11. That's how pathetic I am.

Appropriate or inappropriate?

_____

_____

# END OF CHAPTER REVIEW

In this chapter, you've learned about striking a balance between a formal and informal tone. You've discovered the importance of discovering your voice. You've learned about the importance of detail selection. You've admitted that not all humor is made equal, and that you should almost certainly dial back the fart jokes.

Make a mark on each of the following scales to indicate what kind of voice you currently have. After each scale, note whether you want to shift your voice at all, and if yes, how you might do so.

**My Tone**

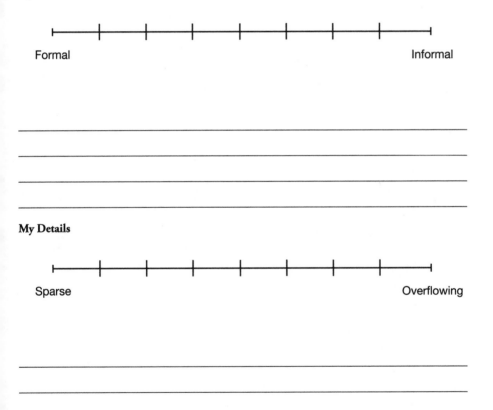

Formal          Informal

_____

_____

_____

_____

**My Details**

Sparse         Overflowing

_____

_____

_____

_____

**My Humor**

Serious ⊢—┼—┼—┼—┼—┼—┼—┼—⊣ Funny

_____

_____

_____

_____

# Chapter 5: Knowing Your Drafts

## How to Refine Your Essay and Make the Final Draft Shine

In this chapter, we will focus on taking your draft from good to great. By the time you have finished this chapter, you should know:

- who will edit your essay

- how you can best incorporate feedback

- what common errors to look for

# EDITING: AN OVERVIEW

Congratulations! You've made it over one of the biggest hurdles in essay writing: putting your ideas onto a page. Completing an initial draft is a daunting first step, but now it's time to put on your editor hat. Editing is vital to the revision process because you want to make sure that your key points are clear to others. Even if English is their first language, many students make it hard for admissions officers to understand them. We recommend that, in addition to reviewing the essay yourself, you enlist the help of some outside sources.

It doesn't matter how good your essay is if no one can understand it.

## ACTIVITY

### What I Meant Was...

Some people find it's easier to edit work that isn't their own. Act as a fresh set of eyes for this introduction and follow along with the edits to see how you can apply similar tactics and observations to your own work. Let's look at a short sample.

> Some people are more curious than others. You aren't satisfied
> with a simple explanations. They must know how and why they are
> scientists.

**What is wrong with this introduction?**

_____

_____

_____

_____

Now look at what this introduction looks like AFTER editing.

> Everybody is curious. Some people are more curious than others.
>
> They aren't satisfied with a simple explanation. They must know how
>
> and why. They are scientists.

**What specific changes made this introduction stronger? Why did those changes have such a positive effect?**

_____

_____

_____

_____

**What can YOU do to avoid leaving mistakes in your own essay?**

_____

_____

_____

_____

For comparison, here are some of our best answers to the last question.

- Ask someone else to edit your essay.

- Edit your essay multiple times.

- Make sure your writing is clear and direct.

 Do not rely on spell-check. That's an external tool that comes at the start of your editing process, not the end. You'll still want to check everything yourself.

# OVERALL DRAFTING ADVICE

Before you start the editing process, there are a few overall rules that will make it as easy as possible to turn your first draft into a great personal essay:

- **It's easier to cut than to add.**

  The first draft of your essay should be a bit too long. You will find that, as you work through this chapter, you will end up revising or removing much of your original text. You don't want to be in a situation where, after making cuts, you're now under the minimum word count.

- **Rome wasn't built in a day.**

  It took Thomas Edison over a thousand tries to create the first lightbulb. Hopefully, your essay will not need as many attempts, but be prepared to write and rewrite this essay many times. The best essays go through a ton of drafts and editors. Give yourself plenty of time for this process.

- **Let it sit.**

  When you are done with a draft, wait at least two days before you go back and edit it again. This will allow you to look at the essay with fresh eyes and see errors that you might otherwise have overlooked. Similarly, when you think your essay is ready to send in, put it aside for a week before a final edit.

- **Don't be afraid to start over.**

  If you have been stuck editing the same portions of your essay over and over again without any improvement, it may be time to choose a different topic that you feel more comfortable with. Alternatively, stick with what you've chosen, but take an entirely new approach to that story.

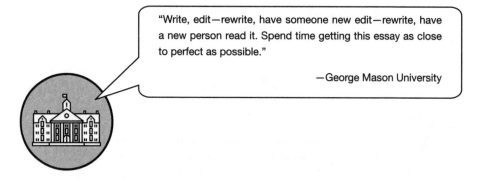

"Write, edit—rewrite, have someone new edit—rewrite, have a new person read it. Spend time getting this essay as close to perfect as possible."

—George Mason University

# FINDING THE RIGHT EDITORS

"I would recommend that all college essays be read by a teacher and another source. So many issues could easily be avoided."

—Moravian College

Set down this book for a moment and go browse through some social media posts—it's okay, we're giving you permission. (But don't take too long!)

Now that you're back (welcome!), think about the number of grammatical errors you spotted along the way and the types of posts in which those were more prevalent. It's likely that the personal accounts you browsed were more prone to making mistakes, whereas the professional accounts—like those of news organizations—were likely to be more carefully worded. Now, the admissions officers *are* looking for a personal statement, but they *do* expect it to demonstrate a certain level of professionalism, so follow in the footsteps of the professionals and make sure at least one other pair of eyes is looking over what you're submitting.

The information you send to colleges shouldn't be at the level of a tweet—imagine having to tell them everything they needed to know about you in 280 characters! So, set the emoji or GIF keyboard down and get yourself a reliable editor who can help you impress the admissions officers.

## Should I ask someone who knows me?

There are both upsides and downsides to asking someone you know to edit your essay. Someone you know will be more likely to know the story that you are telling, understand the context, and be able to help you come up with other personal experiences to use. But they may also fill in blanks in your essay with their own knowledge. That's okay, though; there is no reason to limit yourself to only one editor. In fact, the more quality editors you have, the better your essay will be.

Don't be afraid to use multiple editors! The voice and the work should remain your own, but more eyes can help you catch errors.

# What should I look for in an editor?

Every reader brings something different to the table, so here's a handy guide to why each of the following types of readers can give you valuable, and different, feedback.

| | ✓ Pro | ✗ Con |
|---|---|---|
| **Professional Editors** | They will have a great understanding of what a good personal statement should look like and how to improve yours. | They'll likely cost money. |
| **Counselors** | They will definitely be well informed and impartial. They are likely behind only the professional editors in expertise. | They may not know you well enough to tell if the essay is a good representation of you. |
| **Teachers** | English and History teachers are especially good at helping with grammar and structure. | They may not know what colleges are looking for. |
| **Friends/Family** | Your friends are likely the ones who know you best, and can valuably assess if you're being honest or not. | The advice of those who love you will be good-intentioned, but may not be correct. |

Unconditional love from family is great, but when you're editing, what you need most is tough love. Make sure you don't just pick people who are going to be nice to you, or you may wind up with a perfectly sweet, perfectly forgettable essay.

---

**Professional Editors**

There are many companies that offer professional editing services for the college essay. If you feel that your group of editors is not sufficient, this may be an idea worth pursuing. (Not to toot our own horn, but you can find our services at princetonreview.com/college-admissions/college-essay-review.)

---

# ACTIVITY

## Brainstorm: Who Should You Ask to Edit Your Essay?

Based on what you've learned so far, identify two people to edit your essay. Ask yourself the following questions to get the wheels turning:

**Who are the five best writers that you know?**

**What teachers did the most to make you a better writer?**

**Who are the five people that know you better than anyone else?**

**Do you know anyone who works at a college admissions office?**

Fill in the names of your editors on the lines below.

_____

_____

_____

_____

_____

_____

# ✏ SUPPLEMENTAL ESSAYS ✏

All that we have discussed about editors also applies to the supplemental essay. Your supplemental essay should have multiple editors and should go through several drafts.

But when selecting editors, there is one more question that you should add to the list of questions on page 121.

**Do you know anyone who went to that college?**

Alumni will have a great inside view of the college that will make them great editors. They will be able to tell you whether your essay sounds generic or whether any real passion comes through. They may also have some great specific ideas that you can use to improve your essay.

# MAKING THE MOST OF YOUR EDITORS

Once you have your editors, you'll need to send them your essay so that they can mark it up and give you feedback. But you may also want to prompt them to look for specific things, especially if they have differing areas of expertise, so that you can get the most out of them. After all, you don't just want them to run the same sort of spell-check that your word processing software can do!

## Ask Them About More than Just the Grammar

You don't want to overwhelm your editors—they're doing you a favor, after all. But believe it or not, you'll actually be helping them if you provide them with a list of questions to think about *as* they read the essay. By all means, encourage your editors to give you separate feedback if they have any, but these targeted lists of questions will help them help you, and that's what any good editor wants to do.

- What is the main idea of the essay?
- Did it answer the question?
- Based on this essay, what do you know about me?
- What did this essay do well?
- Did the introduction catch your attention?
- How was the conclusion?

These questions will help you tackle the big picture and make sure that you essay is not just well written but also successful.

# ACTIVITY

Now that you've had some distance from writing a draft of your own essay, reread it and see how you would evaluate its current state.

**What is the main idea of the essay?**

_____

**Did it answer the question?**

_____

**Based on this essay, what do you know about me?**

_____

_____

**What did this essay do well?**

_____

_____

**Did the introduction catch your attention?**

_____

_____

**How was the conclusion?**

_____

_____

# INCORPORATING FEEDBACK

You will get a lot of valuable input by having different people review your essay, especially from non-traditional sources who can see things others don't. However, there are some cases where your editors may give you advice that is at odds with your other editors. When in doubt, listen to the professionals: college counselors, college admissions officers, and books like this..

Not all of your editors will be professionals who know the college admissions process inside and out. When taking advice from family and friends, remember to listen to the experts when in doubt.

Here are some examples of common suggestions from editors that you should NOT take.

## You Can't Write About How You Had Trouble in [middle school]!

Yes, you can! In fact, many good essays feature some kind of struggle and/or growth. You should come across as a person, but not as a perfect one. But if you do talk about how you had trouble organizing your schedule in middle school, for example, there should be some sign of growth. If your essay could be summed up as "I used to be disorganized, I still am, and I have done nothing to work on that," that is going to be a hard sell.

## Why Didn't You Say Anything About Your [chemistry medal]?

Because it has nothing to do with this story. Remember, this is not a list of achievements, this is a personal statement. All of that important information about chemistry medals, soccer championships, or even *Fortnite* rankings should be listed elsewhere in your application. You do not need to repeat it here, unless it is directly tied to your personal statement.

## That's Too Personal! You Can't Write About That!

Yes, you can! Yes, you should! The more specific and personal your essay is, the better it will be.

# You Can't Use Humor!

As we discussed in the previous chapter, you can use humor, you just have to be very careful. Check with a number of readers to make sure that your joke is actually funny and recognizable in the context of the essay as a joke. If your joke could be considered in any way bigoted or offensive, get rid of it.

# You Can't Talk About [politics]!

You'll usually hear this when referring to religion and politics, but it also comes up when dealing with addiction or mental health issues. Yes, you can discuss these topics, but tread carefully. If you are talking about your experience volunteering for a political campaign or working for Habitat for Humanity, that is great. This is not, however, the place for your political manifesto, a thing that would show only one very small facet of your personality. Focus instead on your experiences and what they have meant to you.

# Formal Essays Are Supposed to Be in the Third-Person!

Not this one. It's a PERSONAl essay, and it's awfully hard to get yourself in there as a person without the use of "I" or "me."

Make sure you distinguish between feedback *you* disagree with or that you feel would require a lot of work, and feedback that the reader doesn't have expertise in.

There's an old saying to the effect of "You know it when you see it." The quality of a good editor is being able to *explain* what that something is. The people reviewing your work may not always be able to articulate their reasoning or to convince you, but they've always got a good intention behind flagging something.

You should absolutely follow up with an editor if you're confused, but even if you ultimately disagree with the comment made about a given sentence or paragraph, consider leaving that text underlined, and come back to it another day with fresh eyes. Now, without considering any other comments, make sure the sentence reads well and that it flows and connects with everything around it. You may discover the very thing that makes the sentence feel off.

"Be true to your voice and be very judicious about incorporating editorial advice from friends and parents. It's your essay."

—Connecticut College

# STAGES OF EDITING

If you were on a sinking ship—the *Titanic*, for example—would you take time to make sure that the deck chairs were properly stowed before making your way to the lifeboats? Of course not, and when you're working on your essay, you shouldn't be worry about whether to use a period or a semi-colon until *after* you've made sure that the overall personal statement is answering the actual prompt.

This type of editing is known as triage—start by fixing the most critical issues before you move on to issues with any individual lines.

In short, you don't need to, and probably shouldn't, try to fix everything in your essay in a single pass. You'll probably end up missing things that way! Instead, make a list of the things you most need to focus on, and address some of those first. Repeat the process on draft after draft until there's nothing left to fix. You can use more than the following three stages of editing, but it's a good framework to start from.

## ❶ The Big Picture

These will be your earliest drafts. You should be focused on making sure that your essay answers the question, that it is clear, and that you come across as a likeable and desirable candidate.

Make sure that your essay is clear and focused on answering the question.

## ❷ The Medium Picture

Once you have the basics nailed down, you can start focusing on the introduction and conclusion to make your solid essay much stronger.

## ❸ The Small Picture

This is where you are going to sand down the last rough edges of your essay. You should be focusing on all of the small grammatical errors that spell-check tends not to catch. This is also where you can do a final review for wordiness, repetition, and varied vocabulary and sentence structure.

Just as your own editing should go through these steps, you should have your editors looking for different things at different stages. For example, it may make sense to have your college counselor be one of the first people to read your essay, as they know more than most about the issues you should be focused on in the Big Picture stage.

# FOCUSING ON THE BIG PICTURE

Before you worry about specifics, you need to make sure that your essay accomplishes what you want it to accomplish!

## ACTIVITY

### Pre-Editing Checklist

Think about your essay goals and develop a unique checklist to help get you there.

- [ ] _____
- [ ] _____
- [ ] _____
- [ ] _____
- [ ] _____
- [ ] _____
- [ ] _____
- [ ] _____

# Going from Good to Great

Many people associate editing with only identifying and fixing things that are bad. However, editing is great way to call out sentences or ideas that are effective and well-done. Give yourself a pat on the back and work on developing these already strong sections to turn your essay from good to great.

Don't just look through your essay to get rid of the bad parts. Find the parts of your essay that are especially strong and expand on them.

# ACTIVITY
## Where Have All the Good Lines Gone?

Go through your essay and underline the three parts of it that you feel are most effective. These can be as little as a really good turn of phrase or as large as a paragraph.

If you have not yet written a draft, or if you just want to practice before working on your own essay, look for the three most effective parts of the essay below.

*Note: The prompt was to make up a question that is personally relevant, state it clearly, and answer it. The student below posed the question: What areas are you particularly interested in studying and why? How did your interests develop?*

Everybody is curious. Some people are more than others. They aren't satisfied with a simple explanation. They must know how and why. They are scientists.

Some people think it's irrelevant how or why the world works just so long as it does. Content not to think too hard, they miss out on the sheer wonder that is the world around them. Scientists, on the other hand, learn something amazing every day.

I first began to think about a future in natural science as a seventh-grader when I started a book called *Hyperspace*, by physicist Michio

Kaku. I was somewhat familiar with science fiction staples like black holes, time travel, parallel universes, and higher dimensions, but only as plot devices on Star Trek. A lot of it was beyond my grasp, since I had never taken a physics class, but I had always been interested in the concepts. To think that real scientists seriously theorized about any of it inspired me to read on.

I turned to *The Physics of Star Trek*, which considered the possibility (or not) of the many novelties of the show (like the holodeck, warp drive, and matter transporter) actually existing within the confines of the physical world. Physics seemed a wonderful adventure, so naturally I couldn't wait for my first physics course in high school.

I had to survive chemistry first. At my school, chemistry was considered the most difficult subject around. I didn't have much trouble with it, so I enrolled for a second year to prepare for the AP exam. Concurrently, I took physics and a required semester of biochemistry. I wondered at times if I was nuts to do so, but I braved the elements and was fascinated by what chemistry had to offer: a background for interpreting natural happenings and a means to advance scientific understanding in general, a worthwhile pursuit.

The AP in chemistry required not only a wealth of knowledge, but also an abundance of lab work. I grew confident working with the techniques and equipment and always looked forward to working in the lab. Concepts were one thing, but demonstrating them in the lab provided a whole new insight into what made things work and introduced us to many lab techniques and approaches. Investigations into enzyme performance revealed the effects of various influences; countless titrations of solutions perfected our methods; gel electrophoresis and qualitative analysis tested our nerves and concentration. That year, chemistry was my most challenging subject, and it took up a significant portion of my time. But it was also the most reward-ing. Suddenly, it seemed like chemistry could be part of my future. Now, it seems a more and more possible path. In the meantime, I am a school science lab assistant. I want to explore chemistry and chemical engineering, physics, and biochemistry before narrowing my choices. I want to work in the laboratory, either on the pure or applied side of science.

In any case, I will never stop being curious. I'm a scientist.

Next, look at each of the three excerpts that you have underlined and answer the questions below for each.

1. **What makes this more effective than the rest of the essay?**

_____

_____

_____

_____

_____

2. **How can you make the rest of your text as effective as this?**

_____

_____

_____

_____

_____

## The Message Is Clear

Even the best essay ever written won't help you achieve your college admissions goals unless it also addresses your selected prompt. Refer back to your prompt often during the early revision stages to make sure you're answering the question clearly and concisely.

> "Remember that people are reading the essays very quickly, and so make sure that when a reader is done with an essay, they can sum up what they just read in a sentence or a clause."
>
> —Sarah Lawrence College

## Be Likeable

You've probably heard this before: "It's not what you say, but how you say it." With the college essay, however, *what* you say might actually be more important. Admissions officers will certainly look at your coherence and grammar, but the most cleanly written and compelling essay won't get you anywhere if what it's communicating is alarming.

To put it another way, the essay you're writing serves as a self-portrait. It should be interesting, detailed, and *positive*. You do not want to present yourself in a manner that will make colleges believe that you will be a liability to their institution. In certain cases, this is really obvious. Writing an essay on your love for bullying people on Facebook is an obvious example, but there are more subtle ways that students can trip themselves up. Here are few things to avoid.

**Nobody wants a lecture.** Do you have very strong feelings about climate change, economic policy, or the correct way to load a dishwasher? Great! Do you have a very strong urge to tell your reader what they should be doing about climate change, economic policy, or the correct way to load a dishwasher? Not great. Focus on what you have done and what you think and feel, not what others should do.

**Don't be condescending.** Be careful how you portray those you disagree with, as you never know who is reading your essay. This most often happens in essays dealing with politics or religion. Once again, keep it focused on you and your actions.

**Where's the person?** It's hard to come across as a likeable person if you don't come across as a person at all. This is not a list of achievements and not a manifesto, it is a chance for colleges to get a more complete idea of who you are as a person to balance out all of your grades and other raw data.

# More Common Errors to Avoid

**Saying that something changed your life.**   Don't say this, show this! Often, students will talk about how important an event was in their life without ever discussing specifics. How did you feel during the event itself? What specifically changed? Can you use specific anecdotes to show who you were before, who you are now, and how they differ? For example, instead of writing a play-by-play history of the soccer championship, write about what you were feeling in the moment, why that game was especially important to you, or how that game served as the pinnacle of years of hard work.

**Too perfect.**   If the conclusion of your essay could be summed up as "they all lived happily after," you may have a problem. Also, if you appear to be completely perfect, you have not shown them a complex person. The best essays include things like ongoing struggles, doubt, and failure because it is nearly impossible to show growth without it. It is far better to be honestly real than perfectly fake. If you are writing an essay about your struggles with organization in middle and early high school, it should end with the recognition that, though you have made progress, there is still work to be done. If that essay leaves the reader with the impression that you used to have a problem with organization, but now you have completely overcome the problem, your essay is too perfect.

**Too whiny.**   The struggle can be real, and it's fine to talk about the disadvantages you've had to contend with. But this essay isn't meant to be an excuse for any personal failings, nor is it a pity party. Write that stuff out of your system and then remember that what your reader is looking for is *growth*. This doesn't mean that you've totally overcome all obstacles and adversities (again, avoid being too perfect), but it does mean that you've had accomplishments.

Avoid essays where you talk about what other people do to you and focus instead on what YOU do. For example, instead of talking about how everyone is mean to you, refocus on how you've struggled to make friends. Once you've identified the issue, point out some positives that have resulted from that, or steps that you've taken. For instance, perhaps not having a large social circle resulted in having more free time, time in which you did a lot of reading and perhaps started an online book club or a review blog.

Do you see the difference? In one scenario, you're a passive observer, having things done to you. In the other, you're an active participant, taking charge of a bad situation. Which of those two people is more interesting to you?

# ACTIVITY

Look at the sample below. Underline actions done by the writer and circle actions done *to* the writer *by* others.

> I have always had a hard time reading. When I was very young, I
> was diagnosed with dyslexia. But even with that diagnosis, several of
> my teachers made me read out loud in class. My fellow students made
> fun of me because I couldn't do it. Luckily, my mother complained to
> the principal, so those teachers stopped harassing me.

Revise the circled lines so that they're more active.

_____

_____

_____

_____

_____

Brainstorm some steps that you might have been able to take in this situation.

_____

_____

_____

# Help! My Essay Isn't Personal Enough

Have the last few pages made you realize that your essay needs more of you in it? Let's look at some ways to do that.

## Be Specific

The more specific your essay is, the easier it is to reveal your personality. Having trouble expressing how much your relationship with your grandfather means to you? Use one of your most meaningful memories of him and go into depth. Why is this an important memory to you? How did you feel at the time? Then use these specifics to talk about larger themes, like your relationship with your grandfather as a whole.

## Use Action Verbs

Compare these two statements:

- The bus was gone before I came downstairs.

- I ran down the stairs as fast as I could and burst out the door, skipping breakfast. As I threw down my bag in dismay, I could just see the bus fading into the distance.

Both give us the same information, but the second statement shows us a picture of the author.

## Don't Tell, Show

Always show the action, don't describe it. For example, *I had a hard time after my parent's divorce* does not tell me much about the writer. *When my parents got divorced, I thought the world had ended. Where would I live? Who would I live with? If they could stop loving each other, would they stop loving me next?* Yes, it's a bit melodramatic, but in the second case, we can see much more of what the author feels and fears.

Congratulations, you are almost done with the Big Picture! Before you move on, check your essay for each of the Big Picture errors we discussed.

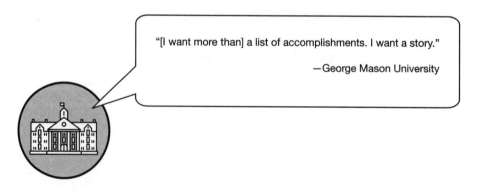

"[I want more than] a list of accomplishments. I want a story."

—George Mason University

# ACTIVITY

## A Literal Big Picture

Draw a literal "big picture" for the ideas in your essay. To do so, begin by choosing the most important word from each sentence of your essay. (If you haven't yet written yours, feel free to refer back to the sample essay on page 128.) Write them below.

_____

_____

_____

Now, think about what you're trying to convey with your essay, and, choosing only from the list of key words below, make a picture out of them. Find ways to circle or connect words that go together, and make the most important words in that list bigger, while making the least important words smaller. Your final image will show how you've associated these ideas and assigned importance to them. Use this "big picture" to make sure that your essay is successfully focused on the same things.

# FOCUSING ON THE MEDIUM PICTURE

In this stage, we are going to focus on the two parts of your essay that can have a very large impact on the quality of your essay: the introduction and the conclusion.

## Introductions

Stop what you're doing. Pay very close attention. Don't look behind you. There is a monster in the room.

No, just kidding. But that grabbed you, didn't it? (The text, not the imaginary monster!) This is what a good introduction should do: immediately hook the reader. Basically, after reading the first few sentences, your reader should want to read what comes next. We will look at what makes good and bad introductions, and what you can do to spice up yours.

## Conclusions

Good conclusions should leave your readers feeling satisfied and connect the essay to a larger theme. We will look at what makes good and bad conclusions, and what you can do to take yours from bad to good.

## Start With a Bang

Let's start off by looking at the introduction below.

| This is a very personable, relatable way to start. |
|---|

[excerpt] So I'm sitting on my couch, wrapped in a blanket that I have somehow wrestled from my sister, enthralled by the electrifying activities taking place before me. The movie is *Outbreak*, and our star, Dustin Hoffman, is in the middle of a standoff with his superior officer, Donald Sutherland. Their argument centers on a certain town in California, contaminated with a certain deadly yet suddenly curable virus, and a plane carrying a chemical agent that will wipe out the entire population of the afore-mentioned town. "No!" my sister shrieks. "Don't drop the bomb!" As the plane veers out over the ocean, the missile flies into the crystal-clear waters and creates an immense, mushroom-shaped wave. "All right!" shouts my family, as out of the jubilee rises my tearful cry, "Wait! What about the marine life?!"

| *Outbreak* is a film not all audiences may know, which is why the author must give some context. |
|---|

| This is not only a jarring question that leaves the reader wanting to know more, but also sets up a direct contrast between the priorities of the author's family and her own concerns. |
|---|

## From Sleepy to Riveting

Having some trouble starting strong? Let's look back at some of the ideas from Chapter 3 that you can use here to help improve your introduction.

## Ask an Unexpected Question

A great way to get your readers interested is to ask a question. Look back at the introduction on the previous page for an example. Remember, this should be a question that makes your reader want to know more about you. Make sure that your question actually intrigues and draws in readers.

## In Medias Res

Remember, when you start in the middle of the action, you make it very compelling for a reader to want to know not only how you'll get out of that situation, but how you got into it.

**SAMPLE:**

> I had been dreading this moment for months. But sitting in this
> chair, listening to the principal justly rail at me, I find myself more
> relieved than scared or angry. Six months ago, this all seemed like a
> great idea. I mean, it all made perfect sense then.

## Use a Shocking Statement

A sensational hook is a great way to draw your readers in quickly. Just be careful that your shocking statement isn't going to offend the reader. For example, it's very dramatic to announce your decision to become a vegan by saying "I used to be a murderer, but don't worry, I'm better now," because you're implying that anyone who eats meat *is* a murderer. However, given that one of your readers probably eats meat, it's probably for the best that you don't accuse your reader of being a killer. Catch the audience's attention, but in a way they'll appreciate!

Does this tactic sound familiar to you? It should. Just as you're trying to make a sentence jump out of your essay and grab the reader's attention, so too are you trying to jump out of the pack of other applicants.

## Starting Off on the Wrong Foot

Imagine that your reader is only going to read the first few lines of your essay. Don't waste them on restatements of the topic or by announcing what you're going to do. This is an all too common mistake! Instead, just jump right in!

*Bad:* In this essay, I intend to show how important my work at Habitat for Humanity has been for my personal growth.

*Good:* Out on the unfinished deck we were building for Habitat for Humanity, it felt like it was 120 degrees, and it wasn't even noon. But even as sweaty and dehydrated as I was, I wouldn't have traded my hammer for anything in the world.

*Bad:* Last summer, I worked at the New York Aquarium, and I learned a lot.

*Good:* Have you ever gotten into a staring contest with a dolphin? Because, let me tell you, over the course of my summer working at the New York Aquarium, I learned that dolphins don't mess around.

*Bad:* I have always loved to read, and my books have done a lot to make me who I am.

*Good:* My parents are very important to me, but they aren't half as important as my books.

# ACTIVITY

## Give It A Go

Now you try! Turn these bad introductions into great ones.

*Bad:* I worked as a golf caddy last summer, and it was very challenging.

*Good:*

_____

_____

*Bad:* When I was ten, my parents separated. It was hard for me to come to terms with this.

*Good:*

_____

_____

# In Conclusion

Here's the conclusion to the essay we looked at earlier.

[excerpt] The funny thing about this whole essay is that I don't even want to be a marine biologist. What I really want to study are the Earth Sciences, but the specifics are not important. I learned this summer what it is to be passionate about what you are doing, to have an unchecked enthusiasm for even the dirtiest aspects of your work. To spend your life in the quest for knowledge that could make the world a better place may sound like a lofty goal, but when it's a real possibility, it's utterly amazing. Like any profession there are twists and turns, opportunities for frustration, disappointment, and conflict, but everyone in that lab knows she is doing something she can be proud of and that might help the world better understand how we can save our planet. Now that I have seen the kind of passion and love with which these people work at their jobs, I would never settle for anything less.

> Don't be fooled here. The author is actually saying something very specific, which is that she learned that her passion wasn't limited to marine biology.

> Watch how the essay expands its scope beyond the job itself so as to focus on a view of the author's life and future. It's a clear picture of the applicant.

> This ends with a personal commitment that signals to a reader that this student would be a driven, active member of the campus.

## Leave Them Wanting More

Your conclusion is (obviously) the last part of your personal essay that any admissions people read. Here are some techniques you can use to make sure that you leave them with the best possible impression of you.

## Come Full Circle

The conclusion isn't a separate part of your personal statement. It is the finishing touch. If your earlier paragraphs, particularly the introduction, began with a question, make sure you've answered it, and emphasize that here. Did you start *in medias res*? This is the place to finish that story arc. In short, don't leave the rest of your essay hanging: refer back to where you started.

## Bring Your Story Home

Your essay may travel a lot of ground as it details all the things that you've done. Make sure that you end things by clearly connecting all of those dots to your own growth. In the conclusion above, there is opportunity to refer back to the New York Aquarium. For your essay, did you write about your relationship with a favorite relative? Discuss the continuing effect of this relationship on your life. Did you write about the circumstances that led to you skipping school one day? Emphasize how that experience has affected how you act now.

Your conclusion *isn't* the place to go off on new tangents or to make new connections. If you have more to say or develop elsewhere, go back to your earlier paragraphs and revise, revise, revise. If it helps, think of this as overtime in a game: you're going to use the skills you've already been showcasing to score one last point to put you over the top.

## Humor

A punch line is a good way to end a joke: it wraps up everything that's preceded it. But ending an essay with a joke risks trivializing all the earnest writing you've done to that point. If you do use humor, tread lightly, using it to lighten the mood or show another side of yourself, but without overpowering the importance of what you've shared thus far.

You know the saying, "You only get one chance to make a first impression"? Don't use your conclusion to fix a flawed portrayal—you have time to go back and improve the rest of the essay. Think of it as your *last* chance to emphasize what you want admissions officers to know.

## In Conclusion, My Conclusion

Let's look at some common mistakes to avoid in your conclusion.

## Concluding Words

In conclusion, do not start your conclusion with *In conclusion, In summation, I would like to close by saying, Finally,* or any other version of this. Would you start your essay with *In this introduction*?

## Epic Fail

Don't oversell the importance of a story you're sharing. If you feel the need to tell readers that your conclusion has changed their world forever, and there is no going back, it's probably not true. Keep the focus on how *you* were changed, and recognize how that relates to the world around you. Should you crave hyperbole, this is where a more openly humorous approach might help: just make sure it remains clear to the reader what you're being serious about.

## Happily Never After

Once you have applied the lessons in this chapter to your conclusion, your essay will be perfect, you'll get into your dream school, and you'll become a billionaire before graduation day. This is, of course, ridiculous.

You should be wary of an essay that wraps up too neatly. While you want to show your readers how you have grown, you should be showing them that you are continuing to grow and that there are still things that you need to work on.

## Repetitiveness

Your introduction is a starting point, but it shouldn't just be repeated throughout the rest of the essay. You're using this introduction to begin your essay, not to reiterate other parts of your essay. Make sure the introduction isn't just rephrasing the overall essay.

Did that feel a little . . . repetitive to you? There's a big difference between being intentionally emphatic and accidentally repeating things. Every sentence should serve a purpose, so if your introduction is just summarizing what the rest of the essay will accomplish, try changing the tone or style so that it hooks the reader.

Make sure to look for these errors in your own introduction and conclusion.

# FOCUSING ON THE SMALL PICTURE

Editing your essay is like taking apart a Russian nesting doll. Once you've unpacked the Big and Medium Picture, you can address the smallest doll: the refining edits. From spelling and grammar to wordiness and repetition, now's your chance to address your essay at the most granular level.

Spell-check is where editing begins, not where it ends.

# Check Your Grammar

Look at the following sentences and see if you can figure out what they have in common. (Hint: if you have access to word processing software, try retyping these there).

> *Every year, my town holds an annual Thanksgiving parade.*

> *That being as it may be, I fully support the great efforts made by my close friends at the world's best restaurant, the inimitable McDonalds in lovely downtown Port Chester.*

> *That is the veracity of the situation.*

> *Decked out in red velvet wallpaper, I entered the dim restaurant.*

> *The faculty at my school treated their new principal with disdain.*

In all likelihood, spell check didn't flag any errors in these sentences. They might even have sounded good to you. But keep reading, because in the next section, we'll identify the error of grammar or style lurking within each one.

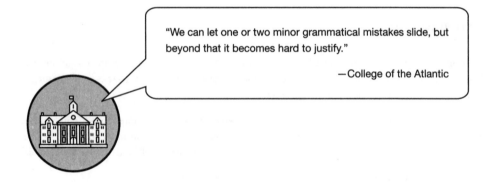

"We can let one or two minor grammatical mistakes slide, but beyond that it becomes hard to justify."

—College of the Atlantic

# Redundancies

 Every year, my town holds an annual Thanksgiving parade.

How often do annual events happen? Every year. That makes this sentence redundant. A better version would be:

 My town holds an annual Thanksgiving parade.

-or-

 Every year, my town holds a Thanksgiving parade.

Repetition is also something you want to look out for at the Medium Picture level, where it takes the form of similar ideas. At the Small Picture level, repetition occurs with individual words in a sentence or a recurring word in a paragraph. Try to mix things up to show your range and be especially wary of repetition in the conclusion.

Most application essays have both a minimum *and* a maximum word count. Don't feel the need to add more words just to add more words. Every word should count.

## Wordiness

 That being as it may be, I fully support the great efforts made by my close friends at the world's best restaurant, the inimitable McDonald's in lovely downtown Port Chester.

There's a big difference between sounding smart and being smart. For all the words used in the sample sentence—30 of them!—the topic being conveyed is just 7 words long. Even with a maximum of 650 words, that only leaves room for about twenty of these heavy sentences. This reduces the opportunity for you to say anything meaningful.

I like the McDonald's in Port Chester.

Check how many of the words in your sentences have something else describing them. This kind of writing generates a lot of words and very little information, which is exactly what college admissions officers hate most. Eliminate as much of this fluff as possible from your essay.

# Word Choice

 That is the veracity of the situation.

What does veracity mean? If you looked it up, you would find something like "truth." If you wrote *that is the truth of the situation*, the sentence is grammatically correct. But veracity and truth do not have the exact same meaning, and in context, veracity makes no sense here. (It's also wordy!) If you use the thesaurus, make sure that you actually know what the word you selected means.

 That's the truth!

 College admissions officers can tell when a writer has used a thesaurus. That sense can take them right out of the essay, as they start thinking about *why* you chose certain words as opposed to thinking about *what* those words say about you.

# Modifiers

 Decked out in red velvet wallpaper, I entered the dim restaurant.

As far as formal English grammar goes, the first noun following an introductory phrase like *decked out in red velvet wallpaper* is what that phrase modifies. So, as this sentence is written, *I am wearing red velvet wallpaper*. But logically we know that it is the restaurant that is decked out.

 I entered the dim restaurant, which was decked out in red velvet wallpaper.

This is the correct version of the sentence. Not all introductory modifying phrases modify the wrong thing, but take a closer look at any in your own essay.

# Pronouns

 The faculty at my school treated their new principal with disdain.

In general, pronouns should agree with their antecedent—that is, the thing they're referring to—and so the word *faculty* should take the singular pronoun.

 The faculty at my school treated its new principle with disdain.

If such rewrites sound off or inefficient to you, or you're not sure which pronoun to use, try rephrasing the sentence:

 The teachers at my school treated their new principal with disdain.

## Sentence Structure

There's one other common mistake to be on the lookout for, and this one can be harder to spot because it's not found in a single sentence. Take a look at the following sentences:

 I went to the store. I went home after that.
I went to sleep about an hour later.

Do you notice that all three sentences are basically the same thing? Each one is just *I went* _____. That kind of writing is most useful as a sleep aid for insomniacs. Let's look at a better version.

 After I went to the store, I drove home. It was about an
hour after that before I went to sleep.

When trying to vary your sentence structure, try changing up the verbs and combining sentences. Another big mistake that people make is writing sentences that are too convoluted (think the *wordiness* sentence). Always be direct and clear.

## More Grammar

Be aware that specific grammar guidelines can vary from school to school, with some being VERY formal in their interpretation of English grammar. As in, some of them still don't believe in starting a sentence with a conjunction. But in general, follow the basic style guidelines of an organization like the Modern Language Association (MLA) or a book like *The Chicago Manual of Style*, and you will be fine.

Check out the grammar appendix on page 207 for even more common grammar errors to keep an eye out for.

# ACTIVITY

Can you spot any errors in these sentences? Not all sentences contain errors.

1. **Swinging from branch to branch, the banana was picked up by the chimpanzee.**

   How would you fix it? _____

2. **Everyone who knows my friends have heard the story about the lobster.**

   How would you fix it? _____

3. **The teachers at my new school have had a positive effect on my understanding of the material.**

   How would you fix it? _____

4. **Joe buys clothes at Walmart because their prices are better than Target.**

   How would you fix it? _____

5. **Although my corgi is very smart, he has trouble understanding Calculus.**

   How would you fix it? _____

6. **In my own personal opinion, the college admissions process is really way too time consuming and has a ridiculous number of steps that need to be completed.**

   How would you fix it? _____

7. **In math class, I continually find myself disinterested; my teacher is just so boring.**

   How would you fix it? _____

**Turn to page 148 for the answers.**

# ACTIVITY

Don't be afraid to start over. If you have worked through several drafts, but your essay is not improving, go back and try again. Don't think of this as wasting time! You're learning what not to do and how to strengthen your writing skills at the same time. More importantly, by shifting gears, you're actually wasting less time than you would if you kept trying to fit this square essay into a round submission.

Here's a test to figure out if you're headed in the wrong direction:

❶ Write your main idea below. Put the number of minutes it took you to state your main idea in the box.

_____

_____

❷ Write what you accomplished in your most recent draft. Put the number of drafts you've done so far in the box.

_____

_____

❸ Pick one sentence at random from each of your paragraphs. Write one of them below. Count the total number of extraneous words and put them in the box.

_____

_____

(continued)

**❹** How many jokes did you use? How many still make you laugh? Put the difference between them in the box.

_____

_____

**❺** List the positive and unique things you wrote about yourself in the personal statement. Subtract this from the total number of paragraphs in your essay and write it in the box.

_____

_____

**❻** Ask each of the people who read your essay to tell you what it was about. Start with 5, and subtract 1 from that number each time a person accurately and positively describes your essay. Write the total in the box.

_____

_____

**Scoring:** If you got between 0–5 points, your essay is in good shape! Stop doubting yourself.

If you scored between 6–11 points, your essay may need some revision.

If you scored 12 points or higher, take a step back and assess whether you know how to move forward. If not, look back to the brainstorming you did, and pick a new topic.

1. Swinging from branch to branch, the chimpanzee picked up the banana.
2. Everyone who knows my friends has heard the story about the lobster.
3. No change! Make sure you know the difference between "affect" and "effect"!
4. Joe buys clothes at Walmart because their prices are better than Target's.
5. No change is necessary!
6. The college admissions process is too time consuming and has too many steps.
7. In math class, I continually find myself uninterested; my teacher is just so boring.

# END OF CHAPTER REVIEW

Let's review the most important takeaways from this chapter.

**You need outside editors.**

List the people you plan on asking to read your essay and what each one brings to the table that's *different* than what the others offer.

| Reader's Name | Occupation | Special Skill |
|---|---|---|
|  |  |  |
|  |  |  |
|  |  |  |
|  |  |  |

**You need to go through several drafts.**

We spoke about the different "Big Picture" levels of your essay. List the ones you plan on using, and what you plan to focus on in each.

**DRAFT 1:** _____

☐ _____

☐ _____

☐ _____


**DRAFT 2:** _____

☐ _____

☐ _____

☐ _____


**DRAFT 3:** _____

☐ _____

☐ _____

☐ _____


**DRAFT 4:** _____

☐ _____

☐ _____

☐ _____


**Do you think you are done? Circle "Yes" or "No."**

## YES                    NO

If you answered "no," put it aside for a day or two and come back to it. If you answered "yes," put your essay aside for one week, and then edit it one last time.

# Chapter 6: Finishing Your Application

## How to Make Sure Your Essay Isn't the Only Thing that Stands Out

Up to this point, you've put a lot of hard work into your personal statement. But none of that will matter if you don't actually *submit* your essay.

In this chapter, we'll look at how to:

- choose which application(s) to fill out

- gather all of the information needed

- accurately fill out the fields

In your normal day-to-day life, you probably interact with people in a variety of ways. You might talk to them face to face, reach them through email or a group chat. The point is, there are multiple ways to get in touch with any one person. The same is true for the colleges that you're applying to. Some may share systems, so if you send your materials to one, you have also sent it to another. Other schools may require you reach out to them in a more specific or direct fashion. As you finalize your list of schools, make sure you know how to most efficiently reach them.

# ACTIVITY

## Ready to Research

The first step to take is to do a little preliminary research. Take your top seven schools and visit their websites to find out which application(s) each one accepts. List them below.

| School Name | Application(s) |
|---|---|
| 1. _____ | 1. _____ |
| 2. _____ | 2. _____ |
| 3. _____ | 3. _____ |
| 4. _____ | 4. _____ |
| 5. _____ | 5. _____ |
| 6. _____ | 6. _____ |
| 7. _____ | 7. _____ |

Look for key commonalities between them. List the application that is accepted by the *most* schools below, and circle the schools that take it above.

_____

Don't discount the schools that you haven't circled. Just be aware that you'll need to do some additional work to apply to those. If you don't think you'll have time, or are you feeling overwhelmed, you may want to more carefully consider where you want to apply.

# TYPES OF APPLICATIONS

All colleges are going to ask you for certain basics:

- personal details about you

- information about your parent/guardian

- your intended major

- your activities

- your grades and applicable test scores

Most will also ask for essays and application letters. Beyond that, the specifics may differ, so look at the following summary of different application types to determine which one—if you have a choice—you want to submit.

If a school accepts multiple types of applications, you can safely choose to submit *any* of the ones on their list. For instance, Harvard, which accepts the Common App, Universal App, and the Coalition App, isn't going to look more favorably at material that comes from one source as opposed to another. Unless you really don't like a particular application's format, choose based on whatever will create the least amount of work for you.

# The Common Application

The name doesn't lie: this is the most common application used by schools, as nearly 900 colleges accept it. It also comes with the most support thanks to its complimentary app, Common App On Track, available for Apple and Android devices.

One key thing to know about this application is that if a school uses it, that school must practice a holistic admissions policy, by which we mean that they promise to factor in your academics, extracurricular activities, and personal qualities as opposed to just judging you by your grades and test scores.

**Website**

Commonapp.org

**Used by**

885+ colleges and universities

**Components**

Personal and Parental Background Information, Courses and Grades, Test Scores, Awards and Activities, Recommendations, Writing Supplements, Additional Information section, Portfolios

**Essay**

Choose 1 of 7 prompts (max. 650 words)

**Help/Support**

Videos, downloadable playbooks, and more resources are available on their website www.commonapp.org/help

**Special Notes**

Holistic admissions

# University of California Application

The University of California system is, in fact, *so* massive that it uses its own application system to cover its nine undergraduate universities. You will note that UCs do not ask explicitly for gender or ethnicity in its application. If you choose to disclose that part of your background, you may do so explicitly in your written responses.

## Website

apply.universityofcalifornia.edu/

## Used by

9 undergraduate UCs: Merced, Irvine, Santa Barbara, Riverside, Santa Cruz, Davis, San Diego, UCLA, Berkeley

## Components

Household Income and family information, Campuses and Majors, Academic History of Courses and Grades, Test Scores, Awards and Activities, Scholarship and Special Programs

## Essay

Choose 4 of 8 personal insight questions (up to 250 words each)

## Help/Support

ucinfo@applyucsupport.net

## Special Notes

Recommendation letters are not accepted (unless specifically requested). Gender and ethnicity are not requested. Until at least 2024, the system is test-optional.

# The Coalition Application

The Coalition Application is one of the newer application systems, put together within the last decade. It aims to be more than an application by offering both a virtual locker that students can start organizing material in as early as 9th grade and a variety of resources to help prepare them for college. The application also focuses recruiters on a student's background more than a student's test scores.

**Website**
www.coalitionforcollegeaccess.org/

**Used by**
140+ Colleges in 34 U.S. States

**Components**
Personal Information, Contact Information, Demographic Information, Use of the Locker, Add Colleges, Invite Contacts for Recommendations and Grade Reports, Activities/Experience, Fee Waiver

**Essay**
Choose 1 of 5 prompts
(500—550 words)

**Help/Support**
mycoalition.help

**Special Notes**
You can opt to start sharing your information with colleges and allow them to text you; You can link your account to the Collegeboard website to share your SAT, Subject tests, APs, and more.

# The Locker

The locker is a cloud-based, digital storage system that allows you to collect, organize, and store your high school work, including papers, photos, videos, projects, art, and even awards. Once the "locker" is created, you can invite your teachers and parents to review its contents and offer feedback about whether the materials will enhance your application. The contents of your locker can be submitted with the Coalition Application. It's a great way to keep track of a graded English paper you did well on, high school activities, class trip photos, and more.

It can be used as a virtual collaboration space, where you can connect with counselors, teachers, and other trusted adults, who can add input to your college application and preparation. Here you can work on college lists, essay ideas, and your applications, among other things.

# Sample Prompt

The prompts on the Coalition Application are designed to focus on the applicant's background. Here's a sample:

- What is the hardest part of being a student now? What's the best part? What advice would you give a sibling or friend (assuming they would listen to you)?

# ApplyTexas

ApplyTexas, as the name implies, is pretty much a one-stop shop for schools in Texas, since all public schools in Texas (and many private ones) can be applied to through its portal. That said, the type of essay that you submit *may* differ depending on the school, so pay close attention to your selections.

### Website
ApplyTexas.org

### Used by
100+ colleges in Texas

### Components
Biographical Information, Educational Background, Educational Information, Test Scores, Residency Information, Extracurricular/Volunteer Activities, Employment Information

### Essay
Up to 3 prompts, each between 350–650 words

### Help/Support
applytexas@austin.utexas.edu

### Special Notes
Depending on your major or the school being applied to, you may have to submit multiple prompts.

## Sample Prompt

ApplyTexas offers three main prompts, labeled A, B, and C, as well as one labeled D that applies only to students majoring in specific artistic fields at certain schools. Of these, C and D are a bit more creative than other prompts you may have seen.

- Topic C: You've got a ticket in your hand—Where will you go? What will you do? What will happen when you get there?

- Topic D: Personal interaction with objects, images and spaces can be so powerful as to change the way one thinks about particular issues or topics. For your intended area of study (architecture, art history, design, studio art, visual art studies/art education), describe an experience where instruction in that area or your personal interaction with an object, image or space effected this type of change in your thinking. What did you do to act upon your new thinking and what have you done to prepare yourself for further study in this area?

If you prefer to look ahead to your future aspirations rather than your past, or if you have been strongly influenced by the arts, these might be ideal prompts for you to address.

# Universal Application

Be aware that the Universal Application is less accepted this year than ever before; as of this book's print date, it was only being accepted by four colleges, all of which also accept other platforms.

### Website

https://www.universalcollegeapp.com/colleges

### Used by

University of Charleston (WV), Cornell University, Harvard College, Notre Dame of Maryland University

### Components

Personal Information, Family Information, Academic Information, Extracurricular Activities, Employment Information, Multimedia Information

### Essay

One personal statement (650 words max.), no prompt provided.

### Help/Support

https://applywithus.kayako.com/uca

### Special Notes

This application does provide room to link to online material that may help to showcase your talents, be it a video, portfolio, song, or article.

# Other Applications

Though University of California's is the biggest, some other large public school systems have their own applications. There are also a few schools, like MIT and Georgetown, that have their own platforms. Note that specialized schools such as these, which have gone to great lengths to set themselves apart, tend only to accept their own application.

# ACTIVITY

## Setting Yourself Up for Success

You may not yet be ready to actually fill out your application, and might not even know which one you're going to be submitting. However, there's no penalty for registering with a site, even if you end up going in a different direction. To make sure that you avoid any pesky technical issues down the road, take some time now to do the following.

First, choose your three favorite applications. Yeah, we know, this is like choosing your favorite medicines, or your favorite tests, but this is a necessary step, so pick an application that will be accepted by the majority (or at least a plurality) of the schools you want to apply to. If a school, such as Harvard, accepts more than one type of application, choose the one that seems most straightforward to you.

_____

_____

_____

Now, visit the website for at least one of those application platforms and create an account for yourself. Make sure you keep track of your log-in information so that you can jump right in when you're actually ready to get started.

Once you're in, browse the interface and take notes about what the application is asking for. Use the following space to note what you already have and what you may still need, and make sure you set yourself up to get anything you're still missing.

| Already Have | Need to Get |
|---|---|
| 1. _____ | 1. _____ |
| 2. _____ | 2. _____ |
| 3. _____ | 3. _____ |
| 4. _____ | 4. _____ |
| 5. _____ | 5. _____ |
| 6. _____ | 6. _____ |
| 7. _____ | 7. _____ |

Now that you know what you need, plan ahead and make sure that anybody else you're going to be reaching out to for help knows what you'll need from them. Whenever others are involved, it's important to leave them enough time to get back to you by the application deadline.

# GATHERING THE MATERIALS FOR YOUR APPLICATION

We've spoken about the various applications you can use to submit your application, and you've gone through and gotten a sense for what material you may still need to gather. Here's a list of some of the big-ticket items that you may need, with room to insert any other more specific elements.

- Transcript(s)

- Activities

  ☐ _____

  ☐ _____

  ☐ _____

- Academic Awards/Accolades/Achievements

  ☐ _____

  ☐ _____

  ☐ _____

- Test Scores

  ☐ _____

      **Test Name**       **Score**

  ☐ _____

      **Test Name**       **Score**

  ☐ _____

      **Test Name**       **Score**

  ☐ _____

      **Test Name**       **Score**

  ☐ _____

      **Test Name**       **Score**

  ☐ _____

      **Test Name**       **Score**

- Parent/Legal Guardian Information

- Digital Locker Information

# ACTIVITY

Don't just use the checklist to keep track of whether you've *gotten* material; make sure you also keep track of *where* that information is. For instance, if you've had test scores sent to schools, note which schools you sent them to so you don't forget to send those scores to additional schools, as well. Space has also been provided to fill in anything that you might need to manually submit.

_____

_____

_____

_____

_____

_____

_____

_____

# Transcript

For most applicants, this is just going to be your high school transcript, which you can request from your school. Note, however, that if you're transferring from a college, you will need to include *both* your high school information and any material from your current college, as well as any summer school programs you may have taken part in elsewhere, but that you want considered for credit and to demonstrate academic rigor.

# Activities

While academics are what get your foot in the door with colleges, it's what you do outside of the classroom that helps build a college campus's community, and that's something admissions officers are always thinking about. This is why most selective colleges practice holistic admissions where they look at your academics, extracurricular activities, your personal qualities, and background. Think of the activities section as a fill-in-the-blank resume of sorts. Extracurricular activities include more than school-sanctioned clubs and teams. Carefully consider how you spend your time outside of the classroom when you're not eating or sleeping.

## Academic Awards/Accolades/Achievements

While activities give schools a good idea of your interests and commitments, awards are an opportunity for you to show how you shine in those activities. This doesn't mean you have to be the MVP of your varsity sports team; being the runner-up or getting an honorable mention, especially in a competitive crowd, is still worth celebrating!

Don't worry about being modest in this section. You're just dutifully reporting on the nice things that *others* have said about you. So long as you don't lie about receiving an award, it's not possible for you to exaggerate.

## Test Scores

Unless you enjoy checking websites over and over again, you'll want to keep track of the scores you've gotten on any tests that you're submitting to colleges—especially if they're required. You'll *also* want to note which schools you've already submitted your scores to for each test: this way, if there are any that still need them, you can request the outstanding scores.

There may be additional fees for sending scores after the test date, so be prepared for those. If a school doesn't require you to officially verify a score until you've accepted admission there, then don't! Your AP scores, for instance, aren't going anywhere, so if a school will let you submit them later, take advantage of that.

## Parent/Legal Guardian Information

You might not know all of this information off the top of your head, or you may have limited information about some members of your family. Fill in the fields to the best of your ability, and where possible, ask your parent/guardian to give you any missing information.

## Digital Locker Information

We spoke briefly about this while discussing the Coalition Application, which comes with a built-in virtual collaboration space in which you can store key information, such as a school research paper that you were especially proud of, or video of a science fair presentation you made, that would be difficult to share in another format. Keep an eye out for schools that accept links to websites or lockers such as ZeeMee, and know that this provides one more chance for you to put yourself over the top with a college admissions officer.

# FILLING OUT THE APPLICATION

As you've probably heard, "Knowing is only half the battle." Once you've gathered all of your information, you will still need to make sure that you include it in the right places. If you've had the misfortune of having to file your own taxes for a summer job, you may already know just how prepared and meticulous you'll have to be with your paperwork and accounting. Here are some of our recommendations.

## Start Early, Finish on Time

You don't have to *finish* early, but by starting earlier, you give yourself a bit of a cushion. You can iron out any technical issues with setting up your account and uploading your information. You can also avoid a last-minute mad dash to complete forms or write your essay, as both of these things can lead to silly errors.

## Know Your Deadlines

Be aware of pressing deadlines for individual parts of your application and make sure you're aware of these up front, so you can focus on them before turning your attention to obtaining information that can be submitted later on.

## Spread Things Out

If the application program that you're using allows you to save your work—and most do—then you don't have to get everything done in one sitting. In fact, we recommend that you don't try to wrap it all up at once. Give yourself time to catch errors! As long as you remain organized, don't misplace documents or forget which ones you've already accounted for, you can take your time.

## Read, and Then Reread, the Directions

Each time you start back up again, make sure that you look at the directions. This is especially important if you're submitting through multiple platforms. You don't want to answer the right question in the wrong portal!

# PUTTING IT ALL TOGETHER

Gather your materials, sit down in a quiet place, take a deep breath, and get started. For sample purposes, we're going to focus on what you can expect to find in the Common Application, but feel free to follow along by looking at the application that you registered for back in the first activity of the chapter. Take note of any differences that you'll need to account for. Also be aware that we're not going to walk through every line—much of what you'll need to fill out on the Common App is, well, stuff that should be common knowledge to the applicant. We will, however, point out tips and strategies where applicable for each section.

 Use the same name on each document you submit. The full legal name you use in your profile should match what's on your test scores, on your transcript, and on any other supplemental information that you submit.

## Profile

The first section of most applications is usually a bunch of personal information that you can recite off the top of your head, since it's about *you*. We're talking things like your legal name, gender, date of birth, contact information, and address. Pay close attention to what is and isn't optional, and where there is and isn't room to elaborate. The Common App provides space to elaborate on gender, if you wish, and certain demographic information such as religion, military status, and ethnicity does *not* have to be provided. By contrast, you must provide information on the language(s) you speak and your citizenship status.

 If any of these optional categories are an important and positive part of who you are, you should share them. It is hard to paint the complete picture of who you are to the admissions readers when you are only using some of the colors.

# Application Fees and Fee Waivers

In the opening section, you will also have the opportunity to apply for a fee waiver, which is essentially a way to ensure that the cost of submitting the Common App does not stand in the way of students who may not be in a place to pay to do so. If any of the following are true, you probably qualify for a fee waiver:

- current eligibility for other fee waivers, like those for the ACT or SAT

- eligible to participate in the Federal Free or Reduced Price Lunch program (FRPL)

    o   Check the income eligibility guidelines set by the USDA Food and Nutrition Service.

- enrollment in a federal, state, or local program that aids students from low-income families (for example, TRIO programs such as Upward Bound)

- living in federally subsidized housing, a foster home, or are currently displaced

- receiving public assistance

- being a ward of the state

If there are other circumstances of note, you can ask a school official, college access counselor, financial aid officer, or community leader to fill out a fee waiver form on your behalf.

# Family

The family section includes several categories for listing the members of your family, their occupations, and their education.

# Education

Colleges aren't trying to trick or trap you when they ask you to list information about your schools and guidance counselors. They're just trying to get the whole picture behind your grades and your courses; learning that you wound up at four different high schools because your family kept moving might help to explain a dip in grades or make above-average scores even more impressive. Also, if you know that a class is AP, honors, Dual-Credit, IB, or the like, make sure that's reflected in the name of the course.

 Note that most applications ask for the courses you're currently taking (or from your most recent year, if you've already graduated). That's why it's a good idea to take some AP-level courses in your junior or senior years, where you can most clearly illustrate a highly valued thing like academic rigor.

## Honors

If you have more than five honors to list here, congratulations! List them all on a separate piece of paper and then, as suggested, add the five that are "most important to you." What that means, exactly, is up for interpretation. You know your own story and achievements, and you can be proud of them regardless of what you put down. Consider prioritizing those accolades that will impress any reader or help you to stand out.

## Community-Based Organizations

If you're not sure whether this section applies to you, set the dropdown to 1 and then scroll through the list of organizations that appears. If you didn't use any of those services, set the dropdown back to 0 and move on.

## Future Plans

It's okay to be undecided here. It's also okay to put something down and later change your mind. Just remember to be consistent throughout your application. If your personal statement talks about your dreams for the future, your answers here should mirror that.

# Testing

In this section, you are given the choice of self-reporting scores or listing upcoming test dates. This is a good option for either letting schools know that you are scheduled to take required tests (or ones that demonstrate academic rigor) or for more cheaply satisfying application requirements. Remember: it costs money to send official score reports, and some colleges don't require anything more than a self-reported score unless they accept you, in which case you can hold off until you've decided to go there.

## Superscoring

Some tests, like the SAT and ACT, give you an opportunity to superscore, which is to submit the highest scores from two (or more) different testing dates. There's no reason not to take advantage of this.

If you are applying to a test-optional school or looking at a non-testing alternative path, you do not have to fill out this section in the same way as other students. Remember, you are demonstrating that you more than fulfill what your college needs, and if scores aren't a part of that, you don't need to stress about them. Do keep in mind that it can sometimes be helpful to include them (if they're good) even if the school doesn't *require* them.

Make sure that you check each school's website for up-to-date information on what sort of information is required. In response to the COVID-19 pandemic, for instance, many schools considered implementing (or did enact) test-optional policies.

# Activities

Don't look at what other students are doing, and don't feel as if there's some sort of perfect list of activities that will help you get into the school of your dreams. So don't force yourself to unhappily play a sport or participate in a club just to put it on your resume. Be especially cautious about overloading your schedule in a way that impacts your grades. Instead of doing community service, serving in student government, and working a part-time job all at once, focus on the activities that you do best, and you'll have a stronger story to tell.

The best way to get into the school of your dreams is for there to be an alignment between *your* dreams and theirs. That is, if you're naturally into activities that the school values, they're going to see you as a good fit.

To put it another way, colleges value quality over quantity and any attempt to do things just to impress a prospective college may backfire. Being in a dozen clubs doesn't matter nearly as much as being on the leadership team for one or two of them.

## Activities for the Common App

Activities are a lot like food; you won't necessarily know which ones you like until you give a bunch of them a taste. Here's a menu, so to speak, of some of the most common ones and some examples of each, but know that this is by no means a comprehensive list. In fact, when you get to college, you'll find that there are often *hundreds* of clubs (depending on the size of the school), so trust us when we say that schools will value any activity that you value.

## ❧ School Clubs ☙

Science Club
Student Council
Spirit Club
JV Soccer
Robotics Club
Key Club
etc.

## ❧ Special Conferences and Programs ☙

Attending Leadership Seminars
Academic Meetings
Athletic Conventions
etc.

## ❧ Recreational and Community-based Organizations and Teams ☙

Baseball League
Religious Group
Mayor's Youth Council
Martial Arts
Music Lessons
etc.

## ❧ Honor Societies ☙

Organizational Work or Planning
Sponsoring/Running Events
etc.

## ❧ Home Responsibilities ☙

Childcare
Eldercare
Family Chores
etc.

## ❧ Self-Study ☙

Online Courses
Experiential Learning
Coding Projects
etc.

## ❧ Work, Internships, Volunteering ☙

Retail Jobs
Summer Internships
Part-Time Employment
Supervised Research
Campaign
Work
etc.

## ❧ Arts ☙

Creative Works in Theater,
Art, Film, Literature,
Dance
etc.

# How To Input Activities on the Common App

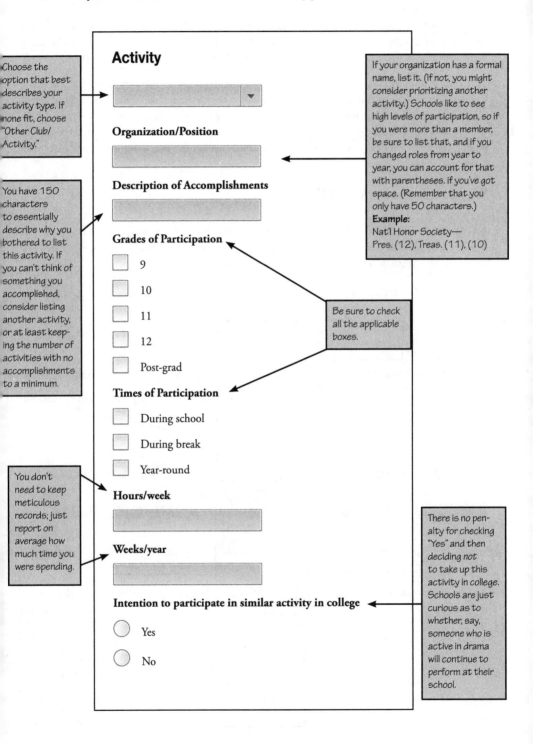

**Activity**

Choose the option that best describes your activity type. If none fit, choose "Other Club/ Activity."

If your organization has a formal name, list it. (If not, you might consider prioritizing another activity.) Schools like to see high levels of participation, so if you were more than a member, be sure to list that, and if you changed roles from year to year, you can account for that with parentheses. if you've got space. (Remember that you only have 50 characters.)
**Example:**
Nat'l Honor Society—
Pres. (12), Treas. (11), (10)

**Organization/Position**

**Description of Accomplishments**

You have 150 characters to essentially describe why you bothered to list this activity. If you can't think of something you accomplished, consider listing another activity, or at least keeping the number of activities with no accomplishments to a minimum.

**Grades of Participation**

☐ 9
☐ 10
☐ 11
☐ 12
☐ Post-grad

Be sure to check all the applicable boxes.

**Times of Participation**

☐ During school
☐ During break
☐ Year-round

You don't need to keep meticulous records; just report on average how much time you were spending.

**Hours/week**

**Weeks/year**

**Intention to participate in similar activity in college**

There is no penalty for checking "Yes" and then deciding not to take up this activity in college. Schools are just curious as to whether, say, someone who is active in drama will continue to perform at their school.

◯ Yes

◯ No

## Once I List an Activity, I Just Can't Stop

You can only list ten activities. This doesn't mean that you need to list ten, and in fact, you shouldn't list random activities that you only participated in for a few weeks. Schools are far more impressed by seeing that you've stuck with an activity for several years, especially if you've made an impact in them.

That said, if you absolutely *have* to squeeze in more than ten activities, or want to fill every available box, consider creative ways in which you might combine or separate similar entries. For instance, if you played on the varsity soccer team and *also* worked with a recreational soccer club, you could put those two together. By contrast, if you played on separate leagues or held more than one position, you could list both. If you do this, though, try to emphasize a difference that justifies your repetition of an activity type.

## Ways to Express Yourself

Let's face it, you've all probably used Twitter before, so the idea of having only 150 characters to sum something up shouldn't be that much of a nightmare. Look at the following descriptions of the same activity to get a sense for how and where you can elaborate.

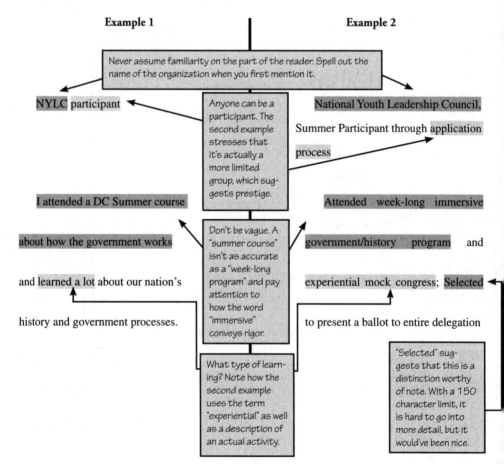

# ACTIVITY

Pick several of the activities on page 170 and see if you can sum them up in 150 characters (or less). Imagine that your audience knows nothing about the process.

_____

_____

_____

_____

_____

_____

Now that you've had a bit of practice, do the same for two of your activities, being careful to avoid acronyms and getting lost in the details.

_____

_____

_____

_____

# Writing Section

You've already learned a lot about how to write the essay throughout this book, so we'll just cover the technical aspect of adding the personal essay to your application. Whether you have to include an essay all comes down to the requirements of the colleges you identified in the "My Colleges" tab of the app, so if you have not already done so, make sure that you do.

If you need to submit an essay, make sure you select the prompt that matches the one you've already chosen, and then paste your finished essay into the box. We do not recommend typing your essay directly into the application because you won't be able to share it with others. You also won't be able to ensure that it saves properly, nor will you be able to use common software functions like spell-check to avoid sloppy mistakes. Write your essay off-platform, share it, edit it, and then paste it into the box provided, and review the finished text one last time to make sure it's formatted properly and that nothing got cut off.

# Courses & Grades

Like the Writing Section, whether you have to list courses and grades on the application depends on the schools you identified in the "My Colleges" tab. Only about 30 colleges require this section to be completed; the rest will simply accept the official transcript(s) from your high school(s).

Having to list your entire high school course schedule is *not* a good reason to remove a dream college from your application list. If it needs to be done—as is the case with the UC and Coalition Applications—it needs to be done. Just pace yourself and don't try to cram in all that information in one fell swoop.

# END OF CHAPTER REVIEW

At the end of the day, only you know how well your application reflects you. Before you click the send button on that application, sleep on it, and really consider if you've exhausted every available opportunity to tell schools about yourself as a candidate. On a scale from 1 (least sure) to 5 (most confident), circle whether the completed application

| | | | | | |
|---|---|---|---|---|---|
| • reflects who I am as a person | 1 | 2 | 3 | 4 | 5 |
| • demonstrates what I care about | 1 | 2 | 3 | 4 | 5 |
| • explains and provides details | 1 | 2 | 3 | 4 | 5 |
| • answers all the questions | 1 | 2 | 3 | 4 | 5 |
| • shares everything that is important to me | 1 | 2 | 3 | 4 | 5 |

# Chapter 7: Going the Extra Mile

## A Guide to Additional Application Submissions that Can Help You Stand Out

You've written, revised, and polished your personal statement. You've analyzed the various applications, gathered all the relevant information, and have completed the forms. And yet you're still worried that you haven't done enough.

In this chapter, we'll look at any extra flourishes you might be able to submit along with your application, such as:

- short-response questions

- letters of recommendation

- supplemental information

- resumes

# SHORT-RESPONSE QUESTIONS

Short-response questions (SRQs) can vary from a list of the websites you visit regularly to your favorite word. They are typically between 50 and 250 words long, although some answers may be as short as five or as long as 650 words. These questions may seem less-critical than a full-length essay; however, EVERY-THING that is on a school's application is there for a reason. No matter how brief and seemingly trivial a query may seem, your answer to each SRQ warrants as much of your attention as a full-length essay would.

## Where Will I Find These?

SRQs are typically found in schools' supplemental essay sections. Some of these responses may be optional, but most are required.

Interpret the word "optional" as mandatory. It's an opportunity to demonstrate your interest in the school and to really give college admissions officers a chance to get to "know" you.

## Common Types of SRQs

There are four types of SRQs you're most likely to encounter on your college applications.

- lists
- words/phrases
- courses you would teach
- anything goes

Let's take a look at each of these categories.

### Lists (150 words or less)

Here's a sample of this kind of prompt, as seen in Columbia's supplemental application.

- List the titles of the required readings from academic courses that you enjoyed most during secondary/high school.
- List the titles of the books, essays, poetry, short stories or plays you read outside of academic courses that you enjoyed most during secondary/high school.

- List the titles of the print or digital publications, websites, journals, podcasts or other content with which you regularly engage.

- List the movies, albums, shows, museums, lectures, events at your school or other entertainments that you enjoyed most during secondary/high school (in person or online).

These are not trick questions. We promise that if a college is asking for a list, they want the answer in a list format, either as a series of bullet points or as an in-line list, with items separated by commas.

Save your paragraphs for the long essays and just be genuine here. If one of your favorite websites is Pinterest.com, list it. If you visit GirlsGoGames.com, list it. If you read the *New York Times* cooking section, list it. If you check your stocks obsessively, include the site you use. Why are schools asking for these lists? Because they reveal your interests and quirks.

Don't leave an admissions officer guessing about what you're referring to. In your lists, write out both the complete title of a book and the author's full name. For a website, include the extension.

When writing your lists, keep the following in mind.

**DO:**

 Choose websites, books, and performances that showcase a range of interests. A school will understand that you like epic Russian literature if you mention something like *War and Peace*, so instead of listing *Crime and Punishment* next, what *else* do you like?

 Keep a list, especially if you find yourself consuming so many things each month that you forget some of them. You may also be able to take inspiration from your class syllabus. That said, if you don't remember something, is it really a favorite?

 Be honest about the art that you enjoy. There's nothing wrong with being a *Harry Potter* or *Hunger Games* fan—in fact, the more specific, the better. Your unique interests will help set you apart, so break out those niche podcasts!

**DON'T:**

 Try to sound overly studious by only listing "smart" or sophisticated responses—admissions will see right through you and know you're being disingenuous. If you loved *Fast & Furious 7*, include it on your list.

 List potentially controversial websites. You don't know your reader's belief system and don't want to alienate admissions by listing a potentially offensive website. Examples of possible landmines: religious or political extremist sites, books, shows, or anything that promotes violence, sexism, or racism. If in doubt, ask a teacher or parent to review your selections.

# ACTIVITY

## Making a List, Checking It Twice

In the space below, free-write anything that you can remember reading, watching, listening to, or visiting in the last six months. Give yourself five minutes.

_____

_____

_____

_____

_____

_____

_____

_____

_____

_____

Go back through your list and put a checkmark next to the entries that you'd want to consume again, or that you really want to talk to other people about. Cross out anything without a checkmark.

Review the list one final time, this time putting a second checkmark next to the entries that you feel would best help someone get to know you and your tastes: it's a bit like making a playlist. Once again, cross out the entries that don't have two checkmarks.

Now, with whatever content still remains on your list, select a prompt from the bulleted list on pages 178 and 179 and complete it.

**Prompt:** _____

_____

**Response:**

_____

_____

_____

_____

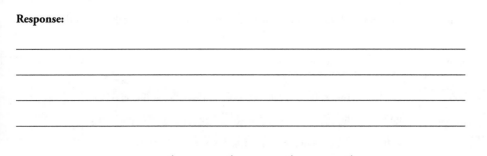

# Words/Phrases (50–250 words)

Some colleges ask students to write brief responses to prompts about words or phrases. These questions seem simple until you realize how few words you're allowed to use. Beware of taking these SRQ's lightly. Write with intent and be genuine. Check out the following examples:

- What's your favorite word and why? (50 words or less)

- What five words best describe you? (Five words)

- List a few words or phrases that describe your ideal college community. (50 words or less)

- Students paint messages on the bridge when they want to share information with our community. What would you paint on the bridge and why is this your message? (250 words)

When answering word or phrase questions in your application, take these tips into consideration.

**DO:**

 Select words or phrases that are evocative and pique your reader's curiosity.

 Use phrases when given the option between words and phrases. You can communicate a stronger message with a group of words rather than a single word.

**DON'T:**

 Use a phrase if the prompt asks for a word.

 Waste precious words in these SRQs by "introducing" your word or phrase with a sentence like, "My favorite word is ..." or "The class I would teach is ..."

Read the following prompt and the accompanying response. See if you can identify any of the elements listed above.

**Prompt:** What's your favorite word and why?

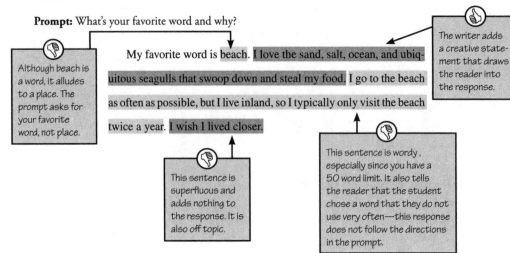

As it stands, the current response is a bit like going to Target for soap, but leaving with popsicles, a yoga mat, and some knick-knacks from the dollar section—and forgetting the soap. Having a word count is akin to having a budget, so just as you have to return the unnecessary items so you can grab the essential soap, so too can your editing "return" those off-topic words until you've gotten back to exactly what you needed.

Similar to rough drafts for longer responses, refining your thoughts to better answer the question will improve your writing immensely. Take a look and see how the writer's SRQ answer differs after a round of editing.

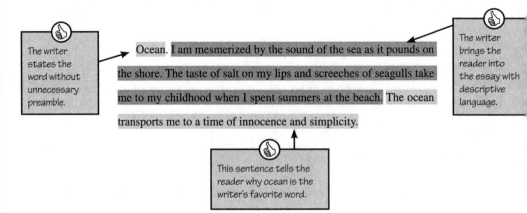

See how much it helped to use the editing strategies you learned in previous chapters? This type of short-response question differs greatly from the longform essay you're used to writing, so to get comfortable writing with such limitations, be sure to actively practice them.

Be deliberate with your language.

# ACTIVITY

### Visual Language

When you're tasked with a limited word count, doing pre-work can help you to better focus on exactly what you want to say.

Fill each of the circles below with one of the words that you would use to answer the Words/Phrases prompt. But don't just write the word! Instead, illustrate it. Use a font that helps to describe your connection to the word or draw a picture in place of one of the letters. This doesn't have to be award-winning art; just try to get how you *feel* down on the page. Then, draw lines out of each circle to three or four new words (you can just plainly write these, unless you feel inspired to keep drawing!) that you would use to describe your connection to that initial word.

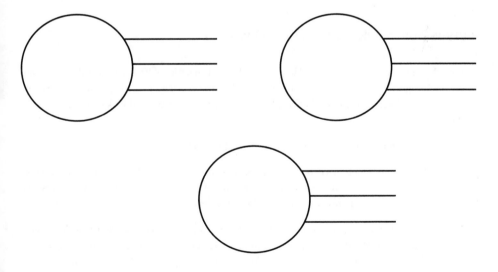

Now that you've created a bank of meaningful words, choose one of the word-based SRQs and try answering it. Build upon what you've already drawn above so that you stay on target.

_____

_____

_____

_____

_____

_____

"I love to see essays that are honest, open without being "too much information," and give me a better sense of who the student is and what they like."

—The University of Chicago

## Courses You Would Teach (35–250 words)

This type of prompt, which has been used by schools like the University of Virginia and Tufts University, is a way for colleges to get a creative response that reveals your priorities in learning, your curiosity, and your ability to write succinctly. Don't be fooled by the brevity of the essay, and make every word count (pun intended!).

- You are teaching a new course. What is it called? (35 words)

- Our Experimental College encourages current students to develop and teach a class for the school community. Previous classes have included those based on personal interests, current events, and more. What would you teach and why? (200–250 words)

- A College X student was inspired to create Flash Seminars, one-time classes which facilitate high-energy discussion about thought provoking topics outside of traditional coursework. If you created a Flash Seminar, what idea would you explore and why? (Approximately 250 words)

If you have to answer one of the prompts, here are some pointers for knocking this response out of the park.

**DO:**

- Be creative! Have fun with your course title.

- Be sincere! Think of a class you would really enjoy teaching.

- Develop a response that reveals both your knowledge and curiosity.

- Stay within the word count. Brevity is part of the challenge in these SRQs.

**DON'T:**

- Try to impress your reader with an overtly technical or sophisticated course title.

- Use complex jargon in your class title or description.

- Waste words by repeating the prompt in the body of your essay.

- Worry that you may not know enough about your topic to teach a class. This prompt is theoretical.

# ACTIVITY

The Of Course Catalogue

The best way to come up with snappy titles for your imaginary courses is to do a little research on some *actual* course titles. You should already be thinking about what courses you'd want to take in college—that's a good way to help narrow down the schools you want to apply to—so start by looking there.

List the five most *interesting* sounding courses below.

1. _____

2. _____

3. _____

4. _____

5. _____

Next, circle the words in each course that draw your attention to them. Is it the specificity of a topic? Is it the alliterative wordplay? Pick a topic and try to generate three *different* potential ways to describe the course. Your final submission should pull from the best elements of each (assuming one of them isn't already perfect).

**Course Topic:** _____

_____

_____

_____

## Anything Goes (100 to 300 words)

For the most part, the prompts that you see have a clear connection to your application, and by now you're getting good at figuring out how to use them to present a clear and vivid picture of yourself as a potential student. Well, this is true even for quirky outlier prompts that may at first seem irrelevant, and that's because they're *not*. Every question has a purpose, even if you can't see it: sometimes a school just wants to see how you'll handle something unexpected.

When you're given a prompt like this, try to respond with the same sort of energy and have fun answering the question.

- What is the hardest part of being a teenager now? What is the best part? What advice would you give to a younger sibling or friend (assuming they would listen to you)? (300 words or less)

- The college admissions process can create anxiety. In an attempt to make it less stressful, please tell us an interesting or amusing story about yourself that you have not already shared in your application. (200–300 words)

- What is your "thing"? What energizes you or engages you so deeply that you lose track of time? Everyone has different passions, obsessions, quirks, inspirations. What are yours? (300 words or less)

- We know you lead a busy life, full of activities, many of which are required of you. Tell us about something you do simply for the pleasure of it. (100 words or fewer)

A bit of a doozy, right? The casual language and personable topics make these feel more appropriate for a conversation with friends, but you're writing to someone who holds your fate in their hands. Don't worry, we've got your back.

**DO:**

 Break down the prompt. Some questions are multi-part, and you need to respond to each component.

 Use lighthearted responses when appropriate. Your application is already full of serious information, so if a school is asking these sorts of questions, they want you to take the opportunity to show them your looser side.

**DON'T:**

 Be sarcastic or humorously address the "difficulty" of answering such a vague question. The school wouldn't ask for this if it didn't want it, so don't devalue the nature of their prompt.

 Make things up. A creative response isn't an excuse for fiction, and it shouldn't require you to brag about or exaggerate your pastimes.

# ACTIVITY

You may have played the game where you fill in the blanks in an unseen story with words so that when you read the finished product, it has a very funny effect. Well, you're not looking for that sort of dissonance here—rather, you want to make sure that the words ring true, but in a creative way. To that end, start by earnestly completing the sentences below with a word or phrase.

1. **The hardest part of being a teenager is** _____.

2. **The most interesting thing I've ever done is**_____.

3. **My most unusual quirk is**_____.

4. **When I have free time, I** _____ **for the pleasure of it.**

Next, take those words or phrases alone, out of context, and rewrite them in a more engaging way. Repeat this a second time, now using the new words or phrases, almost like you're playing a one-person game of telephone.

**Original**          **New Version**          **Third Version**

_____    _____    _____

_____    _____    _____

_____    _____    _____

_____    _____    _____

Now look back at the variations of the phrase, find a compromise, and fill in the blanks with your response.

1. **The hardest part of being a teenager is** _____.

2. **The most interesting thing I've ever done is**_____.

3. **My most unusual quirk is**_____.

4. **When I have free time, I** _____ **for the pleasure of it.**

"I love to see essays that show originality and creativity, and reveal something about an applicant that I may not discover when reading the rest of their application."

—Denison University

# PROGRAM-SPECIFIC REFERENCES

Program-specific references are essay questions that ask about your intended major. Many application platforms are "smart," meaning that the program-specific question appears on the application once you've stated a major or listed yourself as being undeclared.

These essays are a key component of your application. Admissions wants to understand your motivation for selecting a major and your pre-existing commitment to this area of study or, if you're undecided, they want to know what you're considering. As with the SRQs, these prompts tend to be short, with only a few schools allowing for 650 words, so make the most of what you're allotted.

# Examples of Program Specific Questions

As you'll see from the sample prompts below, this type of question is as much about the major you've chosen as it is about how you came to select it.

- Describe a problem related to your area of study, which you would like to solve. Explain its importance to you and what actions you would take to solve this issue. (200 words or less)

- Although you may not yet know what you want to major in, which department or program at College X appeals to you and why? (100 words or fewer)

- Why are you drawn to studying the major you have selected? Please discuss how your interests and related experiences have influenced your choice. (250 word maximum)

- Please tell us more about what has led you to an interest in this field of study, what experiences (if any) you have had in engineering, and what it is about College X's engineering program that appeals to you? (Up to 250 words)

- Describe a significant experience that deepened your interest in studying in the School of Architecture. (300 word maximum)

- Using your personal, academic, or volunteer/work experiences, describe the topics or issues that you care about and why they are important to you. Your response should show us that your interests align with the Business School. (Up to 650 words)

As long as you're responding in good taste, there's not really a wrong answer to these questions, but you do want to highlight your decision-making skills, so be aware of the following best practices.

**DO:**

 Be concise and get to the point right away. Unlike your personal statement, these are not creative writing exercises.

 Research the school's program and hit on key points they mention on the website.

 Answer all of the questions. As with the personal statement, you're not choosing which specific parts to address. Once you pick a prompt, you must answer the whole thing.

**DON'T:**

 Use generic terms or vague language. These prompts are specific and require on-topic responses.

 List the major incorrectly. For example, The School of Engineering and Applied Sciences should not be called The College of Engineering. These names vary from school to school and it's your job to research the major and call it by its official name. This issue is particularly critical when you recycle essays. Make sure you change the major's name for each school.

 Use creative writing. These are short, to the point essays and require program-specific language. You don't have room for extra words or flowery language.

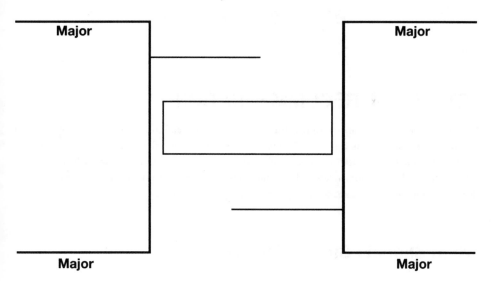

# ACTIVITY

## A Major Melee

First things first: if you don't yet have a major picked out, this might be a good time to try and narrow one down. It'll be easier for you to address this type of question if you *do* have a specific field you want to study, and there's no penalty for changing your major once you are enrolled and attending the school, so try this.

Pick your top four subjects or interests and match them up in a Final Four setting below. The pros should be things that make you excited about studying the subject; your cons should be anything that makes you waver in your commitment. Compare the two for each of the three match-ups and determine which moves on.

Now that you've crowned a major as your "champion," make sure you're referring to it properly. Visit the websites for the schools highest on your list right now and make sure you list exactly how each of them refers to this major.

**Majors of Interest**

Major

Major

Major

Major

College 1: _____     College 3: _____

Major Name: _____     Major Name: _____

_____     _____

_____     _____

_____     _____

_____     _____


College 2: _____     College 4: _____

Major Name: _____     Major Name: _____

_____     _____

_____     _____

_____     _____

_____     _____

# LETTERS OF RECOMMENDATION

Letters of recommendation are typically written by your counselor and core academic teachers to explain why you'll be successful at the institution in question. Some schools also allow elective instructors or non-academic recommenders (mentors, bosses, club advisors, research professors) to submit letters on your behalf. These "other" recommenders address your character and personality in a non-academic context. Because the number of recommenders varies by college, be sure to check your school's requirements.

## When Should I Submit Them?

These letters are submitted with your college applications. This means that you should approach your recommenders well in advance of your personal deadline and the school's deadline. Follow up at least once before letters are due to make sure everything is on track.

# Who Should I Ask to Write Them?

You want to choose people who not only know you well, but who can say good things about you. You also want to make sure that you choose a wide range of recommenders, and that if your chosen schools have any requirements, like needing to hear from a grade- or subject-specific teacher, that you find those as early as possible. Keep in mind the difference, too, between academic references and non-academic ones.

## School Counselor

This one's almost always mandatory, so it helps to try and build a relationship with your school counselor. This person will probably know your hopes and aspirations better than anyone. Your counselor is also likely to have written a lot of these letters over the years; the downside, of course, is that your counselor may already be swamped writing a lot of them *this* year!

## Teacher

Colleges typically request that students provide them with a letter from a core 11th grade teacher, so if you have a great relationship with someone from your first two years of high-school, you might try to take a class with them again your junior or senior year. If you're asking more than one teacher to write a letter, try to pull from different fields: for instance, an English teacher but *also* a math or science teacher.

Be sure that you're only asking those who are likely to say positive things about you. If you got below a B in a course, you may get a mixed letter when ideally you want a glowing recommendation. Find those who can vividly describe your contributions to class and, ideally, also speak to your extra-credit work.

## Employers

The ability to work a part-time job while attending high school speaks highly of your ability not only to multitask but to handle the higher course loads of college—where you may also be doing work-study or research projects on top of everything else. It's good to have letters that show diligence and independence, especially if your employer is able to speak to your growth and how you've personally stood out within the company. Such letters can also add more context to the passions that led you to a specific internship.

# When Should I Reach Out to My Recommenders?

College application season can be overwhelming, even for recommenders, so it's important to give guidance counselors and teachers enough notice if you're interested in receiving a letter from them. Before you begin, double check with your counselor to make sure there's not a special procedure in place for obtaining recommendation letters. If there's not, raise the topic with your select few during the second half of junior year. That way, they can inform you if they prefer to write letters over the summer or in the fall. Also, be sure that you're reaching out far enough in advance such that if one of your intended references declines, you still have time to reach out to alternatives.

# How Should I Ask for Them?

In general, find a time when the person you're reaching out to will be least busy, or hang back after class to ask a teacher when it might be a good time to talk for a few minutes. You don't want to catch someone while they're distracted or preoccupied; that might put them in a bad state of mind when they're considering whether or not to do you this favor. You'd much rather have them feeling flattered and honored that you'd choose them for such an important task.

# What Else Should I Provide?

Time will probably pass between when you first ask if a person would be willing to write a recommendation and when you actually need them to fill out the form. During that period, they may have become distracted or forgetful, and so it can sometimes be helpful to provide teachers with additional information about yourself that they can then choose to highlight in their eventual recommendation. If you are provided with such a form, or a "brag sheet" that asks you to list extracurriculars and awards, complete it as quickly as possible, always leaving your references as much time as possible to then write your recommendation. If you have a resume, you can offer to give that to them as well.

# When Should I Follow Up?

Do your best not to pester someone who has promised to write your recommendation. That said, keep the deadlines in mind. You'll often be able to see in your online application whether a letter has been received from a reference, and if you notice that a due date is nearing and you haven't spoken with that reference in quite some time, it's fair to reach out with a friendly reminder.

Recommendation letters seem complicated, but keep these following best practices in mind to help simplify the process.

**DO:**

 Try to get to know all of your teachers in high school. If possible, spend time outside of class getting extra help or discussing a part of class you found intriguing.

 Write each recommender a thank you note as soon as they write your recommendation. You are notified on the application when the letter is submitted.

 Let your teachers know if you are applying early to your schools so they can write your letter to meet this early deadline.

**DON'T:**

 Wait until the last minute to invite your recommenders. This is insulting and does not acknowledge how valuable their time is.

👎 Involve a teacher who does not meet your college's core requirements. Your school may not want to hear from art, music, or drama teachers, and while you should still use these references as non-academic recommenders, make sure you first cover the scholastic bases.

👎 Ask too many teachers for letters. Two core academics and one or two non-academics are sufficient.

✍ ✍ ✍ ✍

# ACTIVITY

### Who Am I?

Within the image of a student, below, fill in each half with single words that sum up your strengths as a student on one side and as a classmate on the other. Once you've done this, draw arrows out from those individual words to provide short phrases or descriptions that provide more context if needed.

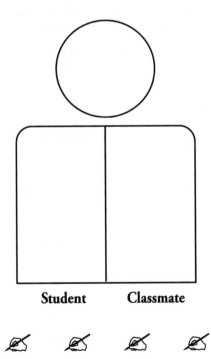

**Student**      **Classmate**

✍ ✍ ✍ ✍

# ADDITIONAL INFORMATION SECTION ON APPLICATIONS

Most college applications include a place for students to add information not covered elsewhere on the form. This is NOT a place for another essay, and there is typically a word limit in this section, so be concise and to the point about *why* you've chosen to mention something.

Here are examples of what's appropriate to include:

- **Special Circumstances:** Were you or your family faced with illnesses, natural disasters, or other challenges that may help to explain an irregularity in your transcript?

- **Unusual Grading:** If your school doesn't use a standard (4.0) or weighted (5.0) GPA, you can provide context to whatever scores have been reported.

- **Lack of Rigor:** Some schools limit the number of AP classes a student can take, when they can take them, or even what honors courses are offered. If your schedule was as demanding as possible, but might not seem that way without a note, be sure to explain it here.

- **Alternative Activities:** If you had limited space in which to describe your activities and awards, or some of them didn't fit existing categorizations on an application (that is, they were listed as Other), this is a chance to discuss them. Don't just use this to list superfluous activities, however; make sure this space is still reserved for highlighting above-and-beyond membership that makes you stand out.

- **Abstracts:** If you've published any papers, collaborated on research, or anything else within the realm of academia, this is a good place to include abstracts or information about such work.

Keep reading for more tips on how to complete the additional informational section.

**DO:**

👍 Use this section to accept responsibility for academic or behavioral challenges in school.

👍 Have a teacher or counselor review your additional information before submitting your application.

👍 Mention an upswing in grades and rigor of curriculum, especially if there is a marked change in your grades.

👍 Explain a high number of excused and/or unexcused absences here.

**DON'T:**

Make excuses for a low grade by writing that you did not get along with the teacher. Either accept personal responsibility for a grade or don't mention it.

Tell admissions how challenging and competitive your high school is in this section. Your school profile will make that apparent (if it is the case).

Copy and paste a resume in this section. Schools that accept resumes will allow you to upload them in their application.

# ACTIVITY

## But Wait, There's More?

Look back at the list of activities you've brainstormed, or at anything you've added to your application thus far. See if there's anything that was left off, or which needs more explanation. If there's anything lingering, any side of you as a candidate that schools have not yet seen and which cannot be added to any existing part of the application, list them below. If not, well, you know the saying: "Speak now, or forever hold your peace."

1. _____

2. _____

3. _____

# SUBMITTING A RESUME

The world's best resume won't make a bit of difference if the college won't accept or look at it. If your resume adds information or perspective on how you spend your time, what you've accomplished, or what's important to you beyond what you've already filled out in the application, consider trying to find other ways in which to convey that information within the bounds of your submission.

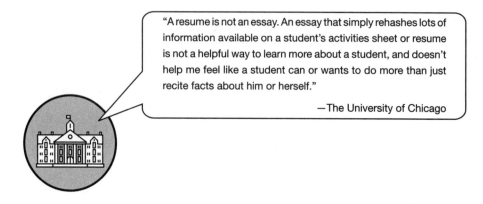

"A resume is not an essay. An essay that simply rehashes lots of information available on a student's activities sheet or resume is not a helpful way to learn more about a student, and doesn't help me feel like a student can or wants to do more than just recite facts about him or herself."

—The University of Chicago

## Mandatory Resumes

Even if a college asks for a resume, that doesn't mean that you should just submit whatever you have, any more than you should just submit any 250–650 word essay for your personal statement. For example, as of the printing of this book, the Cornell School of Hotel Management requests the following:

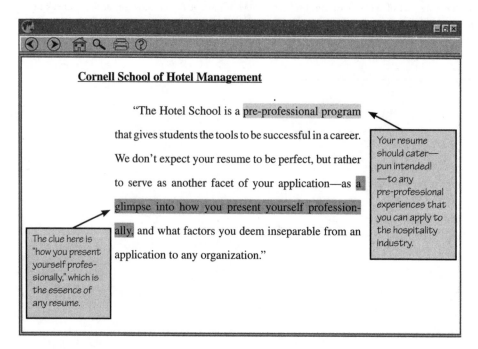

### Cornell School of Hotel Management

"The Hotel School is a pre-professional program that gives students the tools to be successful in a career. We don't expect your resume to be perfect, but rather to serve as another facet of your application—as a glimpse into how you present yourself professionally, and what factors you deem inseparable from an application to any organization."

The clue here is "how you present yourself professionally," which is the essence of any resume.

Your resume should cater—pun intended!—to any pre-professional experiences that you can apply to the hospitality industry.

# Rejected Resumes

It's a lot easier to figure out when a college will *not* accept a resume—at least, it is if you do a little research and visit the school's website. For instance, as of the printing of this book, the University of Virginia states, "We do not accept resumes, research papers, or supplemental application items that do not fit the criteria for arts supplements." Pretty clear, right?

# THE BASIC RESUME

Here's a basic resume template. How do you go from this to a finished product? The same way you get your application submitted: one entry at a time. The main difference is that with a resume, you determine how much to include and how to format it all. That's not an excuse to write a manifesto! Common practice is for your resume to include the most relevant skills for the job (or school) you're applying to—and for the whole thing to ideally fit on one page (or two).

# Your Name

Optional Tagline/summary of your goals or what you care about could go here.

123 Your Street
Your City, ST 12345
**(123) 456-7890**
**no_reply@example.com**

## EDUCATION

**School Name,** Location

Expected Graduation Date
- GPA
- Test Scores
- Type of Curriculum/Can highlight high level courses

## ACTIVITIES

**Organization Name,** Role(s)

MONTH 20XX–PRESENT or you can list your school year of involvement
The number of activities you are trying to highlight will depend on how much space you want this explanation to take up. You can use bullet points, fragments, or a few sentences to highlight the work you did and emphasize any leadership, accolades, initiative, positive results, etc., that you contributed as an individual or a team.

**Organization Name,** Role(s)

MONTH 20XX–MONTH 20XX

See note above

**Organization Name,** Role(s)

MONTH 20XX–MONTH 20XX

See note above

## WORK EXPERIENCE

**Company,** Location—*Job Title*

MONTH 20XX–PRESENT

If you have formal work experience such as retail or customer service work, internships, or research opportunities they can go here. If you don't, just concentrate on the other sections. You can treat this section the same as the activities section and add bullet points or a few sentences to explain your role. If you have unpaid responsibilities such as taking care of siblings or other family members, then you could add them here or in any section you see fit such as an additional information or miscellaneous section.

## PROJECTS

**Project Name**—*Detail*

If you worked on any projects that you are proud of for a school activity, community project or independent study, you can write them here. This could be your IB extended essay, an abstract of your scientific research, a volunteer project you initiated, your GOLD or Eagle Scout projects, and more.

## SKILLS

List quantitative and qualitative AKA hard and soft skills here. You should have at least two skills to list and as many others that fit and seem relevant.

Skill

Skill

## AWARDS

List school, community, other awards or recognition here if you have any. If not, this space can be used for another section such as Additional of Miscellaneous Information, Hobbies, or can extend any of the other sections.

Award

Award

## LANGUAGES

If this is relevant to you and you speak, read, or write another language, you can highlight that here. If English is not your first language and you have taken a TOEFL and IELTS, you could also put those scores here. Languages could also be added to an existing section such as skills or interests.

## INTERESTS

Here you can add hobbies, general or specific interests, or anything else that has not been said in the categories above that is representative of who you are.

Some information is common to all resumes: you'll need to provide contact information, especially if you're submitting this separately from your application.

Though you've likely already covered the bases on education within the application, you should still list your high school(s) and expected graduation date, as they'll add context to the timeline for any work experience or projects you include.

Beyond that, it's up to you how to list your accomplishments. The sample primarily noted work and projects—things that might have been glossed over in your application, and which are of key importance in a resume—but also provided space to discuss skills, awards, languages, and interests.

## Common Guidelines for Resume Writing

**1** Be concise. This is a resume, not a cover letter, so begin each bullet point with an action verb describing your major accomplishments for each item. Do not explain every little detail.

**2** Focus on the activities and accomplishments that you were most committed to. You don't need to account for every hour, so if you tried out a club for a couple of meetings or even a semester but are no longer interested in it, don't feel obligated to add it.

**3** Include necessary details. Make sure the reader knows the name of the organization, your (particularly those in leadership positions), how you contributed to the organization, and any other unique information that you can offer.

**4** Your resume can add new information to your application or go into more detail about an important activity/project you were involved with. You can highlight your passion for art, your just-for-fun coding projects, your love for gardening, or anything else that is part of who you are and what you do.

Admissions officers are looking for tidbits of personal information in your application to get to know you better. Don't be afraid to use the extra space of the resume to share hobbies and favorite things if they'll help the reader better connect with your journey.

**5** Formatting is key but can also be incredibly tedious. Unless formatting is your cup of tea, seriously consider using a free resume template or at least getting an idea of how resumes can look through a quick internet search. Good formatting will result in an easy to read resume, which is clearly divided into sections that highlight your abilities and accolades.

Whether you are writing a resume for a college application or a job in the future, resumes should be easy to read. Admissions officers and recruiters alike will likely spend fewer than 30 seconds reading your resume. Remember to be concise and clear, to quantify or highlight your achievements, and to make the formatting consistent throughout.

**6** Be honest and accurate, without exaggeration. If you have 4 weeks a year where you have to dedicate 40 hours a week to drama club and the rest of the year you contribute about 4 hours, it would be inaccurate to say that you work 40 hours a week on the drama club. Don't misstate job titles either; if you're a co-president, don't needlessly claim to be the president.

Here's an example of that same resume, but filled in for a fictional student.

# Deborah Daniels

I am a passionate high school senior, big sister, daughter, volunteer, thespian, runner, and novice baker looking to find her best fit college and community.

123 Your Street
Sunnydale, CA 94110
**(123) 456-7890**
**Deborah_Daniels@example.com**

## EDUCATION
**Sunnydale High School,** Sunnydale, CA

Fall 2017–Expected Graduation May 2021
- 4.0 Weighted GPA/3.6 unweighted GPA
- SAT 1320 Verbal 700 Math 620
- AP and Honors Courses in Core Subjects

## ACTIVITIES
**Sunnydale High Drama Department,** President (12), Actor (9–12), Tech Crew (9–10)

August 2017–Present
- As President of the Thespian Society, I sit on the selection committee for the 2021 season and mentor underclassmen.
- Acted in 8 plays with 3 lead roles.
- Formally and informally serve on tech crew, building and breaking down sets, and doing whatever is needed.

**Sunnydale Cross Country Team,** JV runner (9-11)

August 2017–May 2020
- Received most improved runner accolade (11).
- I stopped running for the high school this year because of my increased time commitment to drama, but I continue to run several times a week on my own.

**Key Club,** Treasurer (11), Member (10-12)

August 2018–Present
- Planned and participated in several community service events from school cleanups to canned food drives to tutoring elementary school students.
- As Treasurer, I helped guide and plan events for the 2019–2020 school year.

## SUMMER EXPERIENCE
**Sunnydale Community Theater,** Sunnydale, CA—Summer Intern

May 2020–August 2020

- Learned about the inner workings of a community theater by shadowing the Creative Director.
- Participated in staff meetings, helped build and breakdown sets, ran lines with actors, and worked the box office.

**Theater Camp,** Sunnydale, CA—Counselor (unpaid volunteer)

May 2018–August 2018; May 2019–August 2019

- Spent the summers after 9th and 10th grade as a counselor for the Theater Camp I attended for 5 years as a camper.
- Lead kids from all over the city in acting exercises.
- Helped foster a community of openness and silliness throughout the summer and really got the kids to open up and put on a successful and fun show of Peter Pan and Mary Poppins at the end of the summer.

## SKILLS
Builder of inclusive environments especially for kids

Strong public speaker and storyteller

Experienced in Set Design and Theater Production

Sourdough bread maker

Can speak with a convincing Southern Accent

## AWARDS
AP Scholar

Honor Roll (all 4 years)

National Honor Society

Art Honor Society

## INTERESTS
Reading historical fiction novel

Playing Monopoly with my family

Exposing kids to theater

Baking bread

Watching live theater

Working on my British accent

Discovering new arts podcasts

Long, slow runs

# END OF CHAPTER REVIEW

This chapter covered a little bit of many issues you may find on your college applications. From unusual essay question to letters of recommendation and more, hopefully you feel prepared to face it all.

Here's a little game you can play as a reward for completing this book! Below is a College Application Bingo Board. Mark off as many of the squares as you feel comfortable with and see how many ADMITs you can make. If there's anything you haven't yet accomplished, go back and try to fill the entire board!

# A D M I T

| Was proud of something you wrote | Found your writing voice | Researched majors on school websites | Scheduled after school help with a teacher | Asked for a letter of recommendation |
|---|---|---|---|---|
| Diagrammed an "anything goes" prompt | Completed a final draft you were proud of | Changed a "don't" to a "do" in your own writing | Went to a meeting with your guidance counselor | Reached out to a friend, family member, or advisor for help |
| Read recommender requirements for your prospective schools | Edited a SRQ | **Free Space** | Acknowledged your strengths | Showed at least one supplement to a second reader |
| Made your essay less wordy | Participated in a 10-minute brainstorming session | Completed practice exercises | Completed all the activities in this chapter | Made a list of activities and accomplishments |
| Completed all the activities in this book | Restarted on a supplemental prompt | Overcame writer's block | Showed off a side of yourself beyond your academics | Wrote a thank you note |

# Appendix 1: Grammar and Writing Tips

# GOOD GRAMMAR = GOOD FORM

You should strive to make your writing 100 percent grammatically accurate. Think of each essay you write as a building. If it doesn't have structural integrity, admissions officers will tear through it with a wrecking ball.

Let's face it: **Though a thoughtful essay that offers true insight will undoubtedly stand out, it will not receive serious consideration if it's riddled with poor grammar and misspelled words.** It's critical that you avoid grammatical errors. We can't stress this enough. Misspellings, awkward constructions, run-on sentences, and misplaced modifiers cast doubt on your efforts, not to mention your intelligence.

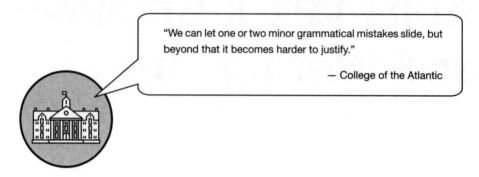

"We can let one or two minor grammatical mistakes slide, but beyond that it becomes harder to justify."

— College of the Atlantic

## Most Common Grammar Mistakes

Chances are you know the difference between a subject and a verb. So we won't spend time here reviewing the basic components of English sentence construction. (If you feel like you could use a refresher, check out our book, *Grammar Smart*.) Instead, we will focus on problems of usage.

Below is a brief overview of the seven most common English usage errors. Knowing what they are will help you remove them from your own writing.

### Mistake #1: Misplaced Modifier

A modifier is a descriptive word or phrase inserted into a sentence to add dimension to the thing it modifies. For example:

*Because he could talk,* Mr. Ed was a unique horse.

*Because he could talk* is the modifying phrase in the sentence. It describes a characteristic of Mr. Ed. Generally speaking, a modifying phrase should be right next to the thing it modifies. If it's not, the meaning of the sentence may change. For example:

Every time he goes to the bathroom outside, John praises his new puppy for being so good.

Who's going to the bathroom outside? In this sentence, it's John. There are laws against that! In order to properly communicate that this is referring to the dog, descriptive phrase *every time he goes to the bathroom outside* needs to be near *puppy*. For instance, "Every time he goes to the bathroom outside, the puppy is praised by John for being so good."

When you are writing sentences that begin with a descriptive phrase followed by a comma, make sure that the thing that comes after the comma is the person or thing being modified.

## Mistake #2: Pronoun Agreement

As you know, a pronoun is a little word that is inserted to represent a noun (*he, she, it, they,* etc.) Pronouns must agree with their nouns. The pronoun that replaces a singular noun must also be singular, and the pronoun that replaces a plural noun must be plural, with one major exception. For the most part, the pronoun "they" can be used to replace "he or she," so if you had a sentence such as "If a writer misuses words, they will not do well on the SAT," it would be acceptable, even though "they," a plural pronoun, is being used with "writer," a singular noun.

This may seem obvious, but it is also the most commonly violated rule in ordinary speech. How often have you heard people say, *The class must hand in their assignment before leaving? Class* is singular. But *their* is plural. *Class* isn't the only tricky noun that sounds singular but is actually plural. Here's a list of "tricky" nouns—technically called collective nouns. These are nouns that typically describe a group of people but are considered singular and therefore need a singular pronoun:

| | |
|---|---|
| Family | Audience |
| Jury | Congregation |
| Group | United States |
| Team | |

If different pronouns are used to refer to the same subject or one pronoun is used to replace another, the pronouns must also agree. The following pronouns are singular:

| | |
|---|---|
| Either | Anyone |
| Neither | No one |
| None | Everyone |
| Each | |

If you are using a pronoun later in a sentence, double-check to make sure it agrees with the noun/pronoun it is replacing.

## Mistake #3: Subject-Verb Agreement

The rule regarding subject-verb agreement is simple: singular with singular, plural with plural. If you are given a singular subject (*he, she, it*), then your verb must also be singular (*is, has, was*).

Sometimes you may not know if a subject is plural or singular, making it tough to determine whether its verb should be plural or singular. (Just go back to our list of collective nouns that sound plural but are really singular.)

Subjects joined by *and* are plural:

Bill and Pat *were* going to the show.

However, nouns joined by *or* can be singular or plural—if the last noun given is singular, then it takes a singular verb; if the last noun given is plural, it takes a plural verb.

Bill or Pat *was* going to get tickets to the show.

When in doubt about whether your subjects and verbs agree, trim the fat! Cross out all the prepositions, commas, adverbs, and adjectives separating your subject from its verb. Stripping the sentence down to its component parts will allow you to quickly see whether your subjects and verbs are in order.

## Mistake #4: Verb Tense

As you know, verbs come in different tenses—for example, *is* is present tense, while *was* is past tense. The other tense you need to know about is "past perfect."

Past perfect refers to some action that happened in the past and was completed (perfected) before another event in the past. For example:

> I had already begun to volunteer at the hospital when I discovered my passion for medicine.

You'll use the past perfect a lot when you describe your accomplishments to admissions officers. For the most part, verb tense should not change within a sentence (e.g., switching from past to present).

## Mistake #5: Parallel Construction

Remember this from your SATs? Just as parallel lines line up with one another, parallelism means that the different parts of a sentence line up in the same way. For example:

> Jose told the career counselor his plan: he will be taking the MCAT, attend medical school, and become a pediatrician.

In this sentence, Jose is going to *be taking, attend*, and *become*. The first verb, *be taking*, is not written in the same form as the other verbs in the series. In other words, it is not parallel. To make this sentence parallel, it should read:

> Jose told the career counselor his plan: he will take the MCAT, attend medical school, and become a pediatrician.

It is common to make errors of parallelism when writing sentences that list actions or items. Be careful.

## Mistake #6: Comparisons

When comparing two things, make sure that you are comparing what can be compared. Sound like double-talk? Look at the following sentence:

> Larry goes shopping at Foodtown because the prices are better than Shoprite.

Sound okay? Well, sorry—it's wrong. As written, this sentence says that the prices at Foodtown are better than Shoprite—the entire store. What Larry means is that the prices at Foodtown are better than the *prices* at Shoprite. You can only compare like things (prices to prices, not prices to stores). To fix this, you would simply need to add a possessive to Shoprite: "Larry goes shopping at Foodtown because the prices are better than Shoprite's."

The word that is used to compare two things is different than the word used to compare more than two things—thanks, English!

**more (for two things) versus most (for more than two)**

Given Alex and David as possible dates, Alex is the more appealing of the two.

In fact, of all the guys I know, Alex is the most attractive.

**less (for two things) versus least (for more than two)**

I am less likely to be chosen than you are.

I am the least likely person to be chosen from the department.

**better (for two things) versus best (for more than two)**

Taking a cab is better than hitchhiking.

My organic chemistry professor is the best professor I have ever had.

**between (for two things) versus among (for more than two)**

Just between you and me, I never liked her anyway.

Among all the people here, no one likes her.

Keep track of what's being compared in a sentence so you don't fall into this grammatical black hole.


## Mistake #7: Diction

Diction means choice of words. There are tons of frequently confused words in the English language that can be broken down into words that sound the same but mean different things (*there, they're, their*), words and phrases that are made up (*refudiate*), and words that are incorrectly used as synonyms (*fewer, less*).

Words that sound the same but mean different things are homonyms. Some examples are:

**there, they're, their:** *There* is used to indicate a location in time or space. *They're* is a contraction of "they are." *Their* is a possessive pronoun.

**it's/its:** It's is a contraction of "it is." Its is a possessive pronoun.

**effect/affect:** *Effect* is the result of something. *Affect* is to influence or change something.

**conscience/conscious:** *Conscience* is a psychological term (Freudian) and is a sense of right or wrong. *Conscious* is to be awake.

**principle/principal:** *Principle* is a value. *Principal* is the person in charge at a school.

**eminent/imminent:** *Eminent* describes a person who is highly regarded. *Imminent* means impending.

Imaginary words tend to crop up from widespread misuse over time, slang usage, or accidental recall. For instance, *alot* isn't actually a word—that would be *a lot*.

In this category are also misremembered words that sound like the real ones, like *refudiate* instead of *repudiate*.

Finally, there are words that are included in dictionaries but which are listed as "nonstandard," like *irregardless*. Unless you're making a point of the usage—that is, showing the reader that you know how *regardless* is the more accepted version—you should stay away from such words.

Sometimes people don't know when to use a word. How often have you seen this sign?

Express checkout: Ten items or less.

Unfortunately, supermarkets across America are making a blatant grammatical error when they post this sign. When items can be counted, you must use the word *fewer*. When something cannot reasonably be counted (like the grains of sand on a beach), you would use the word *less*. For example:

If you eat fewer French fries, you can use less ketchup.

Here are some other words people make the mistake of using interchangeably:

**number/amount:** Use *number* when referring to something that can be counted. Use *amount* when it can not.

**aggravate/irritate:** *Aggravate* and *irritate* are not synonymous. To *aggravate* is to make worse. To *irritate* is to annoy.

**disinterested/uninterested:** Someone who is *disinterested* is impartial, or has an absence of strong feelings—good or bad—about something. A person who is *uninterested*, however, is bored.

Diction errors require someone to cast a keen, fresh eye on your essay because they trick your ear and require focused attention to catch.

Here's a handy chart to help you remember the most common grammar usage errors:

## Grammar Chart

| Grammatical Category | What's the Rule? | Bad Grammar | Good Grammar |
|---|---|---|---|
| Misplaced Modifier | A modifier is a word or phrase that describes something and should go right next to the thing it modifies. | 1. Eaten in Mediterranean countries for centuries, **northern Europeans** viewed the tomato with suspicion.<br><br>2. A **former greenskeeper** now about to become the Masters champion, **tears** welled up in my eyes as I hit my last miraculous shot. | 1. Eaten in Mediterranean countries, the tomato was viewed with suspicion by Northern Europeans.<br><br>2. I was a **former greenskeeper** who was now about to become the Masters champion; **tears** welled up in my eyes as I hit my last miraculous shot. |
| Pronoun Agreement | A pronoun must refer unambiguously to a noun, and it must agree in number with that noun. | 1. Although **brokers** are not permitted to know executive access **codes, they** are widely known.<br><br>2. Unfortunately, both **candidates** for whom I worked sabotaged their own **campaigns** by accepting a **contribution** from illegal **sources.** | 1. Although **brokers** are not permitted to know executive access **codes, the passwords** are widely known.<br><br>2. Unfortunately, both **candidates** for whom I worked sabotaged their own **campaigns** by accepting **contributions** from illegal **sources.** |
| Subject-Verb Agreement | The subject must always agree in number with the verb. Make sure you don't forget what the subject of a sentence is, and don't use the object of a preposition as a subject. | 1. **Each** of the people involved in the extensive renovations **were** engineers.<br><br>2. Federally imposed **restrictions** on the ability to use certain information **has** made life difficult for lawbreakers. | 1. **Each** of the people involved in the extensive renovations **was** an engineer.<br><br>2. Federally imposed **restrictions** on the ability to use certain information **have** made life difficult for lawbreakers. |
| Verb Tense | Always make sure your sentences' tenses match the time frame being discussed. | 1. After he finishes working on his law school essays he **would go** to the party. | 1. After he finishes working on his law school essays he **will go** to the party. |

| Grammatical Category | What's the Rule? | Bad Grammar | Good Grammar |
|---|---|---|---|
| Parallel Construction | Two or more ideas in a single sentence that are parallel need to be similar in grammatical form. | 1. The two main goals of the Eisenhower presidency were a **reduction** of taxes and **to increase** military strength.<br><br>2. **To provide a child** with the skills necessary for survival in modern life is **like guaranteeing their** success. | 1. The two main goals of the Eisenhower presidency were **to reduce** taxes and **to increase** military strength.<br><br>2. **Providing children** with the skills necessary for survival in modern life is **like guaranteeing their** success. |
| Comparisons | You can only compare things that are alike in category. | 1. The **rules** of written English are **more stringent** than spoken **English.**<br><br>2. The **considerations** that led many colleges to impose admissions quotas in the last few decades **are similar to the quotas** imposed in the recent past by large businesses. | 1. The rules of written English are **more stringent than those of** spoken **English.**<br><br>2. The **considerations** that led many colleges to impose admissions quotas in the last few decades **are similar to those** that led large businesses to impose quotas in the recent past. |
| Diction | There are many words that sound the same but mean different things. | 1. Studying had a very positive **affect** on my score.<br><br>2. My high SAT score has positively **effected** the outcome of my college applications. | 1. Studying had a very positive **effect** on my score.<br><br>2. My high SAT score has positively **affected** the outcome of my college applications. |

# Using Punctuation Correctly

Now that we've got that covered, it's time to talk about punctuation, and not the kind that's used for an emoticon.

A formal essay is not like the notes you take in organic chemistry. "W/" is not an acceptable substitute for *with*, and neither is "b/c" for because. Symbols are also not acceptable substitutes for words (@ for *at*, & for *and*, etc.). (In fact, try to avoid the use of "etc."; it is not entirely acceptable in formal writing. Use "and so forth" or "among others" instead.) And please don't indulge in any "cute" spelling ("nite" for *night*, "tho" for *though*). This kind of writing conveys a message that you don't care about your essay. Show the admissions officers how serious you are by eliminating these shortcuts.

Don't leave anything up for misinterpretation; use punctuation wisely and correctly. Here's what you need to know:

## Commas (,)

Very few people understand every rule for proper comma use in the English language.

This lack of understanding leads to two disturbing phenomena: essays without commas and essays with commas everywhere. Here is a quick summary of proper comma use:

**Use Commas to Set Off Introductory Elements.**

- Breezing through my SAT essay, I wondered if everyone were as well-prepared as I.

- Incidentally, I got a "4" on the Writing Sample section.

**Use Commas to Separate Items in a Series.**

- She made hot chocolate, cinnamon toast, scrambled eggs with cheese, and coffee cake.

[Note: There's always great debate as to whether the final serial comma (before the *and*) is necessary. In this case, the comma must be added; otherwise, there will be a question about the contents of the scrambled eggs. In cases where no such ambiguity exists, the extra comma seems superfluous. Use your best judgment. When in doubt, separate all the items in a series with commas.]

**Use a Comma to Separate Independent Clauses.**

Use a comma when the independent clauses are joined by the proper conjunction: for, and, nor, but, yet, so.

- Lindsay ate a big breakfast, but just an hour later, her stomach was still rumbling for more.

**Use Commas Around a Phrase or Clause That Could Be Removed Logically from the Sentence.**

- The Critical Reading section, the first section of the SAT, always makes my palms sweat.

- Xavier, the student whose test was interrupted by marching-band practice, would have liked to have had earplugs.

**Use a Comma to Separate Coordinate (Equally Important) Adjectives. *Do Not* Use a Comma to Separate Noncoordinate Adjectives.**

- It was a dark, stormy night.

- It was a messy triple bypass.

***Do Not* Use a Comma to Separate a Subject and a Verb.**

- incorrect: My new ACT study group, meets at the local café.

- correct: My new ACT study group meets at the local café.

***Do Not* Use a Comma to Separate Compound Subjects or Predicates.**

(A compound subject means two "do-ers"; a compound predicate means two actions done.)

- *incorrect:* My best friend Xavier, and his brother Lou always tell me the truth about my practice essays.

- *correct:* My best friend Xavier and his brother Lou always tell me the truth about my practice essays.

- *incorrect:* Because of the strange tickling in the back of my throat, I stayed in bed, and gave myself a break from studying.

- *correct:* Because of the strange tickling in the back of my throat, I stayed in bed and gave myself a break from studying.

## Colons (:)

Use a colon to introduce an explanation or a list.

- "I think you judge Truman too charitably when you call him a child: he is more like a sweetly vicious old lady." *Tennessee Williams*

- "When I am dead, I hope it may be said: 'His sins were scarlet, but his books were read.'" *Hilaire Belloc*

- "Everything goes by the board to get the book written: honor, pride, decency…" *William Faulkner*

## Semicolons (;)

Use a semicolon to join related independent clauses in a single sentence (a clause is independent if it can logically stand alone).

- "An artist is born kneeling; he fights to stand." *Hortense Calisher*

- "Why had I become a writer in the first place? Because I wasn't fit for society; I didn't fit into the system." *Brian Aldiss*

# Dashes (—)

Use a dash for an abrupt shift. Use a pair of dashes (one on either side) to frame a parenthetical statement that interrupts the sentence. Dashes are more informal than colons.

- "Like a lot of what happens in novels, inspiration is a sort of spontaneous combustion—the oily rags of the head and heart." *Stanley Elkin*

- "Writers should be read—but neither seen nor heard." *Daphne du Maurier*

- "Of all the cants which are canted in this canting world, —though the cant of hypocrites may be the worst, —the cant of criticism is the most tormenting." *Laurence Sterne*

# Apostrophes (')

Use apostrophes in contractions or to show possession. Where you place the apostrophe depends on whether the word is singular or plural (the exception being plural words that don't end with s.) Are you trying to make a word plural? Don't use an apostrophe.

- "Writer's block is only a failure of the ego." *Norman Mailer*

- Karen was proud of her friends' test scores since she knew they had been studying for months.

# Exclamation Points (!)

Use exclamation points sparingly. Try to express excitement, surprise, or rage in the words you choose. A good rule of thumb is *one* exclamation point per essay, at the most.

- "You don't know what it is to stay a whole day with your head in your hands trying to squeeze your unfortunate brain so as to find a word… Ah! I certainly know the agonies of style." *Gustave Flaubert*

# Question Marks (?)

Use a question mark after a direct question. Don't forget to use a question mark after rhetorical questions (ones that you make in the course of argument that you answer yourself).

- "Why shouldn't we quarrel about a word? What is the good of words if they aren't important enough to quarrel over? Why do we choose one word over another if there isn't any difference between them?" *G. K. Chesterton*

# Quotation Marks (" ")

Use quotation marks to indicate a writer's exact words in dialogue or as a citation. Use quotation marks for titles of songs, chapters, essays, articles, or stories—a piece that is part of a larger whole. Periods and commas always go inside the quotation mark. Exclamation points and question marks go inside the quotation mark when they belong to the quotation and not to the larger sentence. Colons, semicolons, and dashes go outside the quotation mark.

- "That's not writing, that's typing." *Truman Capote*

# WRITING CLEARLY

Now that you've gotten a refresher in the building blocks of good writing, it's time to talk about the other half of the equation: style. If grammar and punctuation represent the mechanics of your writing, style represents the choices you make in sentence structure, diction, and figures of speech that reveal your personality to admissions officers. We can't recommend highly enough that you read *The Elements of Style*, by William Strunk Jr., E. B. White, and Roger Angell. This little book is a great investment. Even if you've successfully completed a course or two in composition without it, it will prove invaluable and become your new best friend—and hopefully also your muse.

# Eliminating Wordiness

Remember, good writing is writing that's easily understood. You want to get your point across, not bury it in words. Make your prose clear and direct. **Admissions officers who have to struggle to figure out what you're trying to say might not bother reading further.** Abide by word limits and avoid the pitfall of overwriting. Here are some suggestions that will help clarify your writing by eliminating wordiness.

## Address One Idea at a Time

Don't try to put too much information into one sentence. If you're ever uncertain whether a sentence needs three commas and two semicolons or two colons and a dash, just make it into two separate sentences. Two simple sentences are better than one long, convoluted one. Which of the following examples seems clearer to you?

**Example #1:**

> Many people, politicians for instance, act like they are thinking of the people they represent by the comments made in their speeches, while at the same time they are filling their pockets at the expense of the taxpayers.

**Example #2:**

> Many people appear to be thinking of others, but are actually thinking of themselves. For example, many politicians claim to be thinking of their constituents, but are in fact filling their pockets at the taxpayers' expense.

## Use Fewer Words to Express an Idea

In a 500-word essay, you don't have time to mess around. In an attempt to sound important, many of us "pad" our writing. Always consider whether there's a shorter way to express your thoughts. We are all guilty of some of the following types of clutter:

| Cluttered | Clear |
|---|---|
| due to the fact that | because |
| with the possible exception of | except |
| until such time as | until |
| for the purpose of | for |
| referred to as | called |
| at the present time | now |
| at all times | always |
| in order to | to |

# ACTIVITY

## Eliminating Wordiness

Another way in which unnecessary words may sneak into your writing is through the use of redundant phrases. Pare each phrase listed below down to a single word:

**cooperate together** _____

**resulting effect** _____

**large in size** _____

**absolutely unprecedented** _____

**disappear from sight** _____

**new innovation** _____

**repeat again** _____

**totally unique** _____

**necessary essentials** _____

## Use Fewer Qualifiers

A qualifier is a little phrase we use to cover ourselves. Instead of plainly stating, "Former President Reagan sold arms in exchange for hostages," you might say, "*It's quite possible* that former President Reagan *practically* sold arms in *a kind* of exchange for people who were *basically* hostages." This form of overqualifying weakens your writing, especially in a personal essay in which you should be authoritative enough to firmly assert each point. Prune out these words and expressions wherever possible:

| | |
|---|---|
| kind of | basically |
| a bit | practically |
| sort of | essentially |
| pretty much | in a way |
| rather | quite |

There is also the *personal qualifier*, "in my opinion." This is almost always redundant, and need only be used when it *isn't* clear that you're stating an opinion. If you're using any of the following, try re-reading the sentence without them and see if they can be pruned.

| | |
|---|---|
| to me | it is my belief |
| in my opinion | it is my contention |
| in my experience | the way I see it |
| I think | |

## Use Fewer Adverbs

If you choose the right verb or adjective to begin with, an adverb is often unnecessary.

Use an adverb only if it does useful work in the sentence. It's fine to say "the politician's campaign ran smoothly up to the primaries," because the adverb "smoothly" tells us something important about the running of the campaign. The adverb could be eliminated, however, if the verb were more specific: "The politician's campaign sailed up to the primaries." The combination of the strong verb *and* the adverb, as in "the politician's campaign sailed smoothly up to the primaries," is unnecessary because the adverb does no work. Here are other examples of unnecessary adverbs:

| | |
|---|---|
| very unique | absolutely perfect |
| instantly startled | totally flabbergasted |
| dejectedly slumped | completely undeniable |
| effortlessly easy | |

# ACTIVITY

Rewrite these sentences to make them less wordy.

1. It can be no doubt argued that the availability of dangerous and lethal guns and firearms are in part, to some extent, responsible for the undeniable explosion of violence in our society today.

_____

_____

_____

2. Why is it always imperative and necessary for the teaching educational establishment to subdue and suppress the natural spirits and energies of adolescents in scholarly settings?

_____

_____

_____

3. It seems to me that I believe one must not ignore the fact that Hamlet was a heroic character as well as a tragic and doomed character fated to suffer.

_____

_____

_____

4. No one would deny the strong and truthful fact that young teenage pregnancy is on the rise and is increasing at unbelievable rates each and every single day of the year.

_____

_____

_____

# Eliminating Fragments and Run-Ons

Sentences with too few words are just as annoying to admissions officers as those with too many.

A fragment is an unfinished sentence. It may lack a subject or verb, or it may be a dependent clause. Use this test for sentence fragments: Can the fragment logically stand alone, without the preceding or following sentences?

- *Fragment:* My pencil broke during the last five minutes of the test. Pieces rolling beneath my chair.

- *Correct Sentence:* My pencil broke during the last five minute of the test, and the pieces rolled beneath my chair.

You have to first know the rules before you can break them. You can use fragments to shift the tone of your essay, but that intention must be clear to the reader so that they do not think you've simply made a mistake.

A run-on is an instance where two sentences run together when they should be separate. Sometimes the author forgets the necessary conjunction or the proper punctuation. Sometimes the two sentences are simply too long to fit together well.

- *Run-on:* Regardless of the weather, I will go spearfishing in Bali the water is as clear as glass.

- *Correct Sentence:* Regardless of the weather, I will go spearfishing in Bali, where the water is as clear as glass.

Make sure your sentences don't contain these hard-to-read errors.

# Limiting Your Use of Passive Voice

Consistently writing in the active voice and limiting your use of the passive voice can make your writing more forceful, authoritative, and interesting. Look at the sentences below. They convey essentially the same basic idea, but they have very different effects on the reader.

- The tobacco industry deliberately withheld data about the dangers of secondhand smoke.

- Data about the dangers of secondhand smoke were deliberately withheld [by the tobacco industry].

The first sentence is in the active voice; the second is in the passive voice. The active voice has a clear subject-verb relationship that illustrates that the subject is doing the action. A sentence is in the passive voice when the subject of the sentence is acted upon instead of acting. By distancing the subject from the verb, the passive voice makes it appear that the action is being done to the subject. The passive voice uses a form of *be* (is, am, are, was, were, been) plus the main verb in past participle form. The "do-er" of a passive-voice sentence is either absent or relegated to the end of the sentence in a "by" phrase.

# ACTIVITY

Put each of the following sentences into the active voice:

1. The Constitution was created by the Founders to protect individual rights against the abuse of federal power.

   _____

   _____

   _____

2. Information about the Vietnam War was withheld by the government.

   _____

   _____

   _____

3. The right to privacy was called upon by the Supreme Court to form the foundation of the *Roe v. Wade* decision.

   _____

   _____

   _____

4. Teachers in many school districts are now often required by administrators to "teach to the test."

   _____

   _____

   _____

5. Residents of planned communities are mandated by Block Associations to limit the number of cars parked in their driveways.

_____

_____

_____

6. Mistakes were made by the dancer.

_____

_____

_____

7. The gaze of the tiny porcupine was captured by the headlights of the oncoming Range Rover.

_____

_____

_____

## Using Nonsexist Language

We mentioned earlier that recent shifts in English usage have allowed for the use of *they* or *their* as a means of avoiding *he/she* or *his/her*. (There is, after all, no gender-neutral singular pronoun in English.)

However, using nonsexist language also means finding alternatives for the word *man* when you are referring to humans in general. Instead of *mankind* you can write *humankind* or *humanity*; instead of *mailman*, you can use *mail person*; rather than stating that something is *man-made* you can call it *artificial*.

There are any number of good reasons for you to use nonsexist language, but by far the best is that nonsexist language tends to be more accurate. Some of the people who deliver mail, for example, are female, so you are not describing the real state of affairs by referring to all of the people who deliver your mail as *men*.

If you've been using a word for a long time, like *fireman* instead of *firefighter*, it may feel awkward at first to switch. Practice until it comes to seem natural, as you never know who is going to be reading your work.

# Avoid Clichés Like the Plague

Clichés are comfortable. When we're stuck for the next word, a cliché will suddenly strike us, and we'll feel lucky. We write something like "this *tried and true* method" or "he was one of the *best and brightest*." A cliché may let the writer off the hook, but the reader will be turned off. The reason a cliché is a cliché is because it is overused. Try something original instead of the following overused clichés:

## "I've Always Wanted to Be"

A great personal statement should clearly illustrate the applicant's commitment to and interest in professional goals. Even so, avoid throwaway lines and generic statements that could be repeated by any other wannabe. You'll often see this in conjunction with something like "I've always wanted to be a doctor." Many students who choose to study something as specific as medicine truly feel the decision is the result of a long-term life calling, but making such statements will not distinguish you from the crowd. Instead, it would be better to focus on how you demonstrated that commitment academically and through your activities.

## "I Want to Help People."

Let's be clear: If you really want to spend your life saving lives, then by all means write about it. Just keep in mind that many other people will go this abstract route as well, and not all of them will mean it. As a result of this overuse, many essays about saving lives and healing others risk coming across as bogus and insincere. Even if you're heartfelt, your essay may get tossed into the same pile as all the insincere ones. Admissions officers will take your professed altruistic ambitions (and those of the hundreds of other applicants with identical personal statements) with a sizeable grain of salt. The key is to demonstrate your commitment to public service through examples of the work you have done. If you can in good conscience say that you're committed to a career in the public interest, you must show the committee something tangible on your application and in your essay that will allow them to see your statements as more than hollow assertions.

**Speak from experience, not from desire.** This is exactly where those details we've already discussed come into play. If you can't show that you're already a veteran in the good fight, then don't claim to be. Be forthright. Nothing is as impressive to the reader of a personal statement as the truth.

## Style Chart

| Style Category | What's the Rule? | Bad Style | Good Style |
|---|---|---|---|
| Wordiness | Sentences should not contain any unnecessary words. | 1. The medical school is accepting applications **at this point in time.**<br><br>2. She carries a book bag that is made out of leather **and textured.** | 1. The medical school is accepting applications **now.**<br><br>2. She carries a **textured-leather** book bag. |
| Fragments | Sentence should contain a subject and a verb and express a complete idea. | 1. I went to class. I went to the library. | 1. I went to class and then I went to the library. |
| Run-ons | Sentences that consist of two independent clauses should be joined by the proper conjunction. | 1. The test has a lot of difficult information **in it,** **you should** start studying right away. | 1. The test has a lot of difficult information **in it, so you should** start studying right away. |
| Passive/Active Voice | Choose the active voice, in which the subject performs the action. | 1. **The ball was hit by the bat.**<br><br>2. **My time and money were wasted** trying to keep www.justdillpickles.com afloat single-handedly. | 1. **The bat hit the ball.**<br><br>2. **I wasted time and money** trying to keep www.justdillpickles.com afloat single-handedly. |
| Nonsexist Language | Sentences should not contain any gender bias. | 1. A professor should correct **his** students' papers according to the preset guidelines.<br><br>2. From the beginning of time, **mankind** has used language in one way or another.<br><br>3. Are there any **upperclassmen** who would like to help students in their lit classes? | 1. Professors should correct **their** students' papers according to the preset guidelines.<br><br>2. From the beginning of time, **humans** have used language in one way or another.<br><br>3. Are there any **seniors** who would like to help students in their lit classes? |

# Navigating the Minefield

Besides grammatical concerns, students should keep in mind the following points while writing their admissions essays.

## Don't Repeat Information from Other Parts of Your Application

The admissions staff already has your transcripts, standardized test scores, and list of academic and extracurricular achievements. The personal statement is your only opportunity to present all other aspects of yourself in a meaningful way. Even if you don't mind wasting your own time, admissions officers will mind if you waste theirs.

## In General, Avoid Generalities

Admissions officers have to read an unbelievable number of boring essays. You'll find it harder to be boring if you write about particulars. It's the details that stick in a reader's mind.

## Don't Go On at Length About Your Goals

With all respect to you, you're young. Many seemingly single-minded students go on to change their majors and careers throughout both college and their post-graduate life. That's normal! With that in mind, maybe focus a little more on what you've done and what you immediately want to do, and leave your 75-year plan alone for now.

## Maintain the Proper Tone

Your essay should be memorable without being outrageous and easy to read without being too formal or sloppy. When in doubt, err on the formal side.

## Don't Try to Be Funny, Unless What You Have to Say Is Actually Funny

An applicant who can make an admissions officer laugh never gets lost in the shuffle. No one will be able to bear tossing your application into the "reject" pile if you garner a genuine chuckle. But beware! Only a select few are able to pull off humor in this context.

## Stay Away from Anything Even Remotely Off-Color

Avoid profanity. It's not a good idea to be irreverent in admissions essays. Also, there are some things admissions officers don't need (or want) to know about you, so keep those things to yourself.

## Circumvent Political Issues If Possible

Admissions officers don't care about your political perspectives as long as your viewpoints are thoughtful. They don't care what your beliefs are as long as you are committed to the preservation of human life. The problem is that if you write about a political issue, you may come across as the type of person who is intolerant or unwilling to consider other viewpoints. In college (and certainly in your professional career), you'll occasionally be challenged to defend a position with which you disagree—and you don't want to seem like someone who is so impassioned that you are incapable of arguing both sides of an issue. If you opt to write about politics, do so in an open manner, and be careful to avoid close-minded offenses.

"When a student writes in ways that seem to negate others' perspectives as valid, especially with inflammatory language, we may wonder whether this person will be a healthy participant in campus dialogues."

—Sarah Lawrence College

## Consider Your Audience If You Want to Write About Religion

As a general rule, don't make religion the focal point of your essay unless you're applying to a college with a religious affiliation. Don't misunderstand us—religion is not taboo. It's totally fine to mention religion in any personal statement; just make sure to put it within the context of the whole, dynamic person you are.

## No Gimmicks, No Gambles

Avoid tricky stuff. You want to differentiate yourself but not because you are some kind of daredevil. Don't rhyme. Don't write a satire or mocked-up front-page newspaper article. Gimmicky personal statements mostly appear contrived and, as a result, they fall flat, taking you down with them.

# Excuses, Excuses...

Admissions officers have seen every excuse in the book for bad grades and lousy test scores. Rather than make excuses, you want to come across as resolute and capable of doing better.

## "My Test Score Isn't Great, But I'm Just Not a Good Test Taker."

Don't dwell on a low standardized test score in your personal statement. If there were extenuating circumstances, you can briefly mention them, or you can include a separate note in your application. If there were no such circumstances, it's best to avoid mention of your score. There's a reason for the test being taken before entrance to college—it's a primer, the first of many tests that you will take as a student. If you don't take tests well and the SAT or the ACT confirms it, don't make excuses for it; instead, resolve to do better. Consider also that a low standardized test score speaks for itself—all too eloquently. It doesn't need you to speak for it too. The test may be flawed, but don't argue the unfairness of them to admissions officers who use them as a primary factor in their admissions decisions. We feel for you, but you'd be barking up the wrong tree there.

## "My Grades Weren't That High, But . . ."

This issue is a little more complicated than the low test score. If your grades fall below average acceptance criteria to most medical programs, or if there are certain anomalous periods of low achievement on your transcript, it's probably best to offer some form of explanation—especially if you have a good reason for lower performance, such as illness, family issues, or a demanding work schedule. College admissions committees will be more than willing to listen to your interpretation of your high school performance, but only within limits. Keep in mind that schools require official transcripts for a reason. Members of the admissions committee will be aware of your academic credentials even before they read your essay.

**If your grades are unimpressive, the best strategy is to offer the admissions committee something else by which to judge your abilities.** Many admissions committees say that they are willing to consider students whose grades or test scores fall slightly below the average acceptance criteria, particularly if they've demonstrated extraordinary altruism or service to the community. Again, the best argument for looking past your grades is evidence of achievement in another area, whether it is your test score, extracurricular activities, overcoming economic hardship as an undergraduate, or career accomplishments.

# Appendix 2: Sample of Successful Student Essays

The following essays are some of the best that we've seen over the last ten years, and come in response to a variety of both prompts and word counts. Do not, under any circumstances, read these with the intent of copying the structure or, worse, the content.

Instead, read them to be inspired by how each student found a way to tell their truth. Delve into the sentences that you like and figure out what makes them work so that you can go back and give your own writing that same close scrutiny and make sure it's living up to the standards of a successful student essay.

# STUDENT 1

**Prompt:** Describe a place or environment where you are perfectly content. What do you do or experience there, and why is it meaningful to you?

Rather than love, than money, than fame, give me an order of wings.

And a table with my friends.

Stadium Grille isn't the kind of place that would typically inspire a college essay. It's not where I found the cure for cancer or ended world hunger. And it sure doesn't look like Thoreau's cabin in the woods. It's just a neighborhood burger joint. But despite its outward appearance, Stadium Grille is a safe haven for me because it is an escape from everyday life and everyday problems. It is where I am my truest self. It is my Walden.

Stadium Grille is a sports restaurant – a nondescript concrete block building near a strip mall, a few paces from a gas station off a busy suburban highway. It would hardly catch your eye. But it's a sanctuary for the loyal patrons who relax at its sticky tables. It's filled with big screen TVs and serves ribs and pitchers of soda. The air hangs heavy with a mixture of grease and the sweaty uniforms of the local sports teams that congregate there. The kitchen would make a health inspector faint. All of these things lend it a quirky personality that cannot be imitated by a chain restaurant. But what makes Stadium Grille really special – even transcendent – for me is that I go there with the same five or six best friends who all order the same food…at the same table…at the same time every week. In this predictable ritual of buddies lies a peacefulness that is more real and more authentic than anything I could discover in a silent forest. What started as a way to kill time and pick up cheap food has become an almost sacred gathering.

Henry David Thoreau is one of my favorite writers. When I discovered the Transcendentalists in my junior AP English class, something spoke to me – especially when I read Walden. One of my favorite passages is "I wanted to live deep and suck all the marrow out of life." This, of course, has a different meaning for everyone. For Thoreau, it meant living a spare, solitary life; for an avid stamp collector, it might mean assembling the quintessential collection; for a pitcher, throwing that perfect slider. For me, it means retreating to a place where I am among true friends, where I can count on a perfect sameness and where everyone knows my name.

Although I have spent an excessive amount of time and money at "The Grille," I don't consider anything wasted. "Hanging out with friends" is not the kind of thing you can put on a resume. No parents are going to brag about their son's latest trip to Dollar Wing Night. But I don't consider my time there squandered. In fact, Stadium Grille has become an important part of who I am because I always leave happier, more inspired and more clear-minded than when I enter. And despite our casual outward appearance, my friends and I have, in fact, accomplished something important there over the years. We have helped each other grow up.

In the spring of 2010, one friend's father died suddenly. After paying our respects and attending the official services, it wasn't long before we migrated to The Grille. Beneath the trash talk about our favorite sports teams was an almost therapeutic support group for our friend. During a time when everything was changing for him, Stadium Grille was one of the only things that remained the same. He has since thanked us – just for hanging out and being there.

Stadium Grille won't always be my Walden. Someday I will find my safe haven with my wife or children or in a career I am passionate about. But it has been priceless to me because it is one of the first places that I have called Home.

—Robert Langan Watters

# STUDENT 2

**Prompt:** Recount an incident or time when you experienced failure. How did it affect you, and what lessons did you learn?

It has been a challenging road, but I must admit that I have made many sacrifices and have worked intensely to become a new person. For years, I tried to lose weight, but failed to do so. Nevertheless, ironically, I have been experiencing some good "downs" in my life. As the scale keeps going down, I am emotionally going up. Since this significant change in my life began, I have gone through several difficult, but satisfying moments. My emotional and social life, my physical appearance, personality, and lifestyle have all changed. Today, I can enjoy life and feel more secure about myself than ever before. My social life was poor and I did not felt comfortable going out with my friends or meeting new people. Now, I look forward to spend time with friends and even make new ones. The most shocking change I have experienced so far would be my physical appearance; I consider myself a new person. You may find this silly, but even dancing at parties or enjoying going paddle boarding, running, and going to the beach are activities I can now enjoy because of my self-esteem and confidence. Another milestone in this process was when I had to replace all the clothes that did not fit me. I began to celebrate minor goals like achieving my "weight goal of the week". Some people would say that I have changed a lot, and I know I have, but I also think that my "new" personality was always there- hidden under many pounds and many fears. I have become a more interactive and happy person, which now complements my personality. Being overweight did not only affect my body or health, it was excess baggage in my life. My grades and self-esteem were the most affected aspects in my life because of my laziness and lack of motivation; procrastination was my hobby.

I decided to make a change during the summer of 2012. Family and friends helped and motivated me—but the one who persuaded me to make this very important change was my dad. For years he told me that it was not healthy. He had offered me to receive special treatments by doctors and nutritionists, but denial stopped me and had no idea of how serious it was. The first months were very difficult, and the first weeks almost impossible. I had to cut everything that was unhealthy like sugary, and sodium-filled food. One week later, at my first appointment with the doctor, I weighed the same 253 pounds I did when I started. The doctor said that in order for the body to adjust it could take over seven days. The second week, I had lost my first five pounds. I cried, but this time I was very proud of myself. I would have never lost fifty-three pounds without the support of my parents.

This has been a true journey, which has provided great life lessons. I learned that in order to accomplish a goal I have to work and do it not for anyone else, but myself. Working hard, with much effort, good intentions, and inner strength will, certainly, lead me to the expected reward and more. I constantly thought I would fail like before because it was difficult to resist temptation, but I am so glad and proud of myself for not breaking down and, on the contrary, continue pursuing what I had so decided. Most importantly, it has definitely made me realize that failing is necessary to achieve positive results in many aspects of life.

—Gabriela Fernandez Gutierrez

# STUDENT 3

**Prompt:** Describe a personal achievement that you're proud of.

My most important experience was a real delight and an eye-opener which provided me with a memory to last a life time. The experience thought me that in all things of nature, there's always something marvelous. I have never had any reason to doubt this statement because I'm a living proof of it.

I'm an archetypal 18 year old. I'm tall enough for a girl my age; good looking, but not in a Halle Berry kind of way. I'm also a prospective pre-medical student; already have two short story books to my credit, and an aspiring essayist. Why am I singing such praises of myself? Just to explain that the attainment of self complacency comes with a great deal of self knowledge and love. But in order to attain this, one must first learn to accept oneself as one is. That was where my struggle began.

Being born and raised in Africa, I had always taken my African heritage to be as much of a curse as it is a burden. My self loathing was further fuelled when my family had to relocate to the Gulf country of Qatar. The culture shock between the two continents for me was seriously debilitating. I had moved from an all black continent to an all white continent, where the masses were used to people of their own kind. Adjustment to a new culture for me had no meaning because I had to deal with the stigma of being a 'Sudani' in the society, although Sudan was not my home country. I learnt later that a Sudani was simply a person with black skin.

Another factor which contributed to my self dislike was the fact that although I was a good writer, I did not like that fact that I could not speak as flawlessly as Martin Luther King Jr. My stuttering, although not really severe, had succeeded in damping my self confidence and prevented me from enjoying various activities I normally enjoyed. It functioned as my shield, always standing between me and any fine opportunity that came my way. I took it as an excuse to shun any public speaking sessions, lost interest in school speeches and hid comfortably behind its wicked screen. I remember vividly the great panic I had felt before my TOEFL iBT test. I was three days away from my assigned test date and while taking my practice test, I faltered a lot on the speaking section due to my speech disorder and anxiety. My anger erupted and I cursed my whole being with intense passion. I was a nervous wreck. In fact, I had unknowingly let my stuttering tyrannize over me.

Although I was different from the people around me in my city, it wasn't difficult for me to adjust after a while. I attended a high school which had majority of Indians and because of that, I always stood out. The difference for me was very identifiable; like a red, angry gash staring me in the eye and made me feel like my whole being was created differently. For instance, compared to all the Indian girls around me, with their long, black hair and lithe, athletic bodies, I had curly, afro hair and full, red lips. My nose always had a thin sheet of sweat on it no matter what the weather was, and my palm was just a little bit harder than that of the Indians. Due to all these differences, at that time, I always believed that God had made a mistake while creating me or maybe he went on a lunch break.

In addition to my aforementioned differences with other people, I also had other causes to believe that I was a total mistake. For example, I have such an atypical admiration for the legendary voice of Whitney Houston. Among my other friends, I noticed that I was the only one who was always playing her music or watching her music videos. As my friends have always told me, "I don't see why you should give her so much preference; she's no different from Beyonce!" Of course, people's taste in music vary; but for me then, that was just another reason to bury myself further in my shell with the cry "I'm so different!"

As I grew older however, the benefits of being a different person in the society gently unfolded before my eyes. My revelation sought me out one day as I was returning home from school in the school bus. A girl of about eleven was sited in front of me. Her posture and structure were perfect. "Of course, she's Indian," I whispered to myself. The girl suddenly turned back to ask a favor from her friend in the back seat, and my surprise nearly suffocated me. She had a thin sheet of sweat on her nose too, and it was the month of November! "Wow," I whispered to myself; "this isn't a genetic disorder after all. Even if it's only one person that I have seen with this kind of sweating pattern, then it's perfectly normal". Some days later, my life gave another surprising twist. As I was frantically searching the internet for stuttering remedies before my TOEFL iBT examination, I accidentally stumbled onto a website on 'famous people who stutter'. I was a bit relived when I realized that the famous golf player – Tiger Woods also had the same problem! In addition, my mother told me about my uncle whose stutter was worse than mine. The appealing thing about him though, is that he has attained a PhD degree and is a very successful pharmacist. I was further stirred when I learnt that the great scientist, Isaac Newton, and the famous Winston Churchill also had the same stuttering problem. Then it dawned on me – if I'm smart, I don't need my stuttering to stand between me and my success.

Another aspect which helped to boost my self confidence came days later as I was watching the News about Oprah Winfery. My pride and admiration nearly blew my brains apart as I learned of her trials and tribulations and her later attainment of success, riches and world-wide fame. As the Newscaster reported, "She's one of the few female billionaires in history and she's a black woman". Whenever I think of that statement, and my former hatred of my skin color, I practically drown in shame.

Today, however, I smile at my image in the mirror whenever I get the chance because I have grown to appreciate my beautiful, full lips which more than half of Hollywood stars spend millions to acquire. I compliment my lustrous, clear, brown skin and braid my natural afro hair with pride. I have also learnt to accept my speech disorder as a transitory setback and view it as my foundation to a better future. I don't feel ashamed anymore if I have different tastes from people, especially my friends; it simply gives me a feeling of uniqueness. At present, the idea of 'self respect' and 'self understanding' has taken on a new meaning for me because I feel that in order to understand and care for other people, I need to understand and care for myself first.

—Nwamaka Bob-Ume

# STUDENT 4

The beaming lights adjusted their focus on me as I walked toward center stage. Holding my violin and bow, I looked out to the packed audience which seemed to contrast my own solitary position. I had practiced every note in Bach's Sonata No. 2 many times before, yet this performance seemed a daunting task as I hesitantly lifted my violin. In that moment, as I thought about the beauty of the music I could create, nothing else —not even the audience— mattered. All I could do was bring out every ounce of my expression, drop my anxiety, and start the first note with brilliance. Playing the violin is certainly my most valued passion.

To me, the violin is not a separate item that I control, but an extension of my own body, emotions, and thoughts. Music's language of sound has deeply impacted my personality, making me more aware and sensitive to the people around me. In a practical sense, the violin has allowed me to appreciate music in different settings. As a soloist, I have learned the skills and nuance needed to let my ability stand on its own. As part of an orchestra ensemble, I learned the importance of communication and putting the success of the team above myself. Whether I'm playing a sophisticated Mozart or an informal "Rodeo", I always try to put my best talents forward. I am dedicated to bring this same passion as I ascend to my new center stage: Wayne State University.

—Aniruddh Mannari

# STUDENT 5

## Essay 1

---

**Prompt:** Describe a place or environment where you are perfectly content. What do you do or experience there, and why is it meaningful to you?

---

The best classroom I have ever set foot in was a 1995 Dodge Grand Caravan.

Really, there's nothing at all special about that van. In fact, I've always hated it. It's cramped, smells like stale dog, and the upholstery is constantly crusty from God knows what. Despite its faults, that awkward gray box on wheels is where I feel most at home. It is where I learned lessons about my passion, my faith, and everything else essential to my personality from my most important teachers—my family.

My family has always been a catalyst for my passion for math. With a math teacher uncle, an engineering undergrad brother, and an MIT engineer grandfather, math conversation was easy to find, and it never came as often as in that van. My uncle Andrew is a self-proclaimed "prime number enthusiast" (he even created a prime number board game, Prime Time™) and that van was where we connected through our love of math. We played a game where we gave each other three-digit numbers and figured out their prime factorizations. To any non-numberphile, that's probably the most boring game in the world. But the game isn't what was special about those car rides, it was the connection the game brought. I never had the chance to spend much time with my uncle. While I grew up in Maryland, he was for whatever reason raising donkeys in central Georgia, and a few years ago he moved to Winchester, England. With the little time I saw him, our games were how I learned about my uncle. I got to know his sense of humor and the way his mind works. He passed on to me all his little mathematical tricks about prime numbers, squaring numbers, and whatever else I needed, and those tricks are the closest connection we have.

Conversations in that van taught me about another crucial part of myself: my faith. In my hometown of rural Harford County, Maryland, Jews were not exactly well represented. I was Bar Mitzvah'd in a class of seven, and confirmed with only two. Temple Adas Shalom was also too poor to hire a full-time rabbi, so my understanding of Judaism came from car rides to and from synagogue with my mom. I learned the main tenets of my faith, including differences between types of Jews, and Jewish and Christian ideologies. On one ride my mother talked to me about the pillar of Judaism that would define my faith as a whole: Judaism is the religion of asking questions. She taught me that Judaism rewards pursuing higher knowledge and understanding, and that blind acceptance is not the way to spiritual fulfillment. This concept of knowledge through questioning had always been my philosophy outside of worship, but I had never thought to ask questions about my faith. That revelation finally allowed me to connect my faith to my everyday life, and made me want to continue my Jewish education. Together in that dingy van, my mother gave me the opportunity to develop my own ideas about something that will always be a huge part of my life.

That van was where I learned my most essential values. It's where I developed my views on relationships, education, and ethics. It's where I got to communicate with my family on a truly personal level. In past decades, the dinner table has been the watering hole of family dynamics: the place where after a long day, family members would come together and talk to each other free of the outside world. But these days, the only place safe from the distractions of the surrounding world is a tin box on wheels barreling down I-95. I am content where I discuss things I value with people I care about. And if that place is a two-decade-old Dodge Caravan with 130,000 miles on the odometer, then I can't wait for the next road trip.

—Eli Jaffe

# Essay 2

---

**Prompt:** Tell us about a personal quality, talent, accomplishment, contribution or experience that is important to you. What about this quality or accomplishment makes you proud and how does it relate to the person you are?

---

I have always had the ability to perceive and understand another person's state of mind. In the past I used this ability only to avoid conflict, but as I have grown as a person, this ability has enriched every part of my life, including my sense of humor and my relationships.

I was always the peacekeeper of my family. It's in my nature. I avoid conflict because I can see the consequences and weigh them against the costs of conceding. My mom says when my brother and I were both infants, we had two identical strollers. I sat in one and he threw a fit because he wanted that one. She thought it was so amazing when I calmly stood up and sat in the other stroller. That dynamic carried through my entire childhood, but not exclusively with my brother. I took middle seats on long car rides, admitted to wrongful accusations, and took the raw end of every deal. I made every sacrifice to avoid the horrible arguments I saw everyone else endure. At that point in my life, my understanding nature was working against me. I was able to put myself in others' shoes by truly listening to them, but when using that skill to appease others, I was forgetting about my own wants and needs.

Now, I have learned to use my ability to understand others without sacrificing my own happiness, and this skill has helped me in many aspects of my life. One major way I use this skill is with my sense of humor. The most important thing about making a joke is the audience. It doesn't matter how funny I think my joke is if the people around me don't. Since I'm around so many different people, I use my ability to understand others to adjust my jokes. It would be ridiculous to tell the same kind of jokes around my friends as I tell around my grandparents or my teachers. I have a friend Adrian who loves terrible puns, so whenever I have a good one, I bring it to her. My friend Kevin loves jokes about the internet, and my Physics teacher Mr. Sloan loves physical humor (no pun intended). Being able to recognize these qualities in others helps me to foster better relationships and use humor to connect with them on a deeper level.

This skill allows me to connect with others on not only a humorous level, but a conversational level as well. My family contains some of the most stubborn people I have ever met, especially my Grandpa Bob. When I was younger, he and I would argue on and on over the most ridiculous things. We once argued for twenty minutes because he despised Will Ferrell based on his acting roles (I still don't really understand why). However, the most frustrating part is not that he wouldn't concede his point, but that he would make no attempt to try to understand my argument. It is beyond frustrating to try to have an argument or even a conversation with someone who refuses to acknowledge your perspective. Being subjected to arguments with such stubborn people allowed me to recognize when I was being stubborn myself and helped me to better communicate with others. By truly listening to other people's arguments and seeing issues from their perspectives, I can not only get my point across more effectively, but also see sides to issues that I had never considered.

My ability to read and understand others helps me in nearly every facet of my life. In the past it hindered me, making me sacrifice my own happiness to please others. However, it now allows me to form lasting relationships with others through both humor and conversation by seeing the world through their eyes. Connecting with others on this level enriches both my own life and theirs, and what quality could I value more?

—Eli Jaffe

# NOTES

# NOTES

**NOTES**

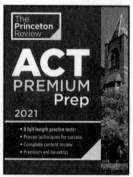

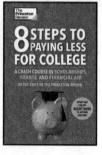